DOCUMENTS OF DISSENT

DOCUMENTS OF DISSENT

Chinese Political Thought since Mao

Translated
with an Introductory Essay by
J. CHESTER CHENG

HOOVER INSTITUTION PRESS
Stanford University, Stanford, California

Hoover Institution Press Publication No. 230
Hoover Institution at Leland Stanford Junior University,
Stanford, California 94305-6003

First printing 1980
23 22 21 20 19 18 17 16   9 8 7 6 5 4 3 2

Manufactured in the United States of America

The paper used in this publication meets the minimum requirements of the American National Standard for Information Sciences—Permanence of Paper for Printed Library Materials, ANSI/NISO Z39.48-1992. ∞

Cataloging-in-Publication Data is available from the Library of Congress.
ISBN-13: 978-0-8179-7302-5 (paper)

To Camilla

When the Prince has faults, admonish Him.
　　　　　　—Mencius

Contents

Acknowledgments

I wish to acknowledge my gratitude to the director, W. Glenn Campbell, and the staff of the Hoover Institution on War, Revolution and Peace for their help throughout my research. I am also indebted to my friends Kung-yi Kao, James J. Y. Liu, Ramon Myers, and Richard Staar of Stanford University for their painstaking advice and helpful suggestions. Many thanks must be conveyed to my own institution, San Francisco State University, and to my family, without whose unstinting support this project would have been impossible.

Introduction

How do informed, intelligent citizens react when a leader of mythical stature like Mao dies and is replaced by an unknown? Like the Soviet Union, information about the People's Republic of China comes only from indirect sources—official documents, travelers' tidbits, and wall posters—sources that shed little light on the inner workings of the communist leadership. We remain woefully ignorant of policymaking and public opinion processes, the formation of intraparty factions, and power struggles in the party, state, and armed forces in China. What are the shared values and competing political viewpoints held by members of the omnipotent Communist Party of China, now led by Chairman Hua Kuo-feng? We simply do not know.

We learn about political change only after events recede into the past. For example, one very remarkable political development of 1976 was the meteoric downfall of a few party activists, the so-called Gang of Four, led by the late Chairman Mao's wife, Chiang Ch'ing. Although based in China's largest city, Shanghai, the Gang of Four appeared to be the personal mouthpiece and supporter of Chairman Mao and his revolutionary policies across the length and breadth of China. In the final phase of the Cultural Revolution, the Gang of Four and its ardent followers not only occupied key party and bureaucratic posts in education, propaganda, culture, and the performing arts, but also extended their influence into the military and trained, equipped, and commanded militia units throughout China. One member of the Gang, Chang Chün-chiao, even became director of the General Political Department of the powerful People's Liberation Army; another, Wang Hung-wen, emerged as vice-chairman of the important Military Commission of the party's Central Committee. Even now, despite the voluminous allegations since their downfall in October 1976, we know little about their past activities other than that they did exist and were perceived as a threat.

As these radicals were ascending to power, other party leaders began to advocate the moderate program of the Four Modernizations of Chinese industry, agriculture, military defense, and science and technology and bitterly opposed the efforts of the radicals to extend their revolutionary ideology into culture, education, and politics. And while radicals and moderates remained locked in struggle, each seeking support from an aged and ailing Chairman Mao, another faction, which may be characterized as conservative, among the leaders doubted the wisdom of China's foreign policy since the worsening of Sino-Soviet relations in the late 1950s, especially the steps taken by Mao himself after 1971 to seek détente with the West.

What do we know about these factions? Who were their leaders, and how numerous were their followers? We know next to nothing. But incontrovertible information that at least enables us to say that such factions did exist surfaced in China in 1976 and 1977.

From mid-1976 until late 1977, Chinese activists surreptitiously sent a few documents to individual scholars and research institutions in the United States. These activists resemble the Soviet *samizdat* writers, and these documents, poorly printed on crude paper, have all the trappings of the underground materials that circulate within the Soviet Union among the privileged few. But these Chinese *samizdat* writers distinguish themselves from their Soviet counterparts by their refusal to utter individual grievances. Instead they passionately argue in earthy language that the socialist revolution in China has been derailed, betrayed if you will. In their moral outrage at the current leaders of China, they denounce China's current foreign policy and its revisionist line.

We can only speculate about the veracity of these *samizdat* papers. They appear to serve the same purpose as the well-known *Ts'an-k'ao hsiao-hsi* (Reference Materials) published within China for top leaders and senior cadres only. But unlike these officially sanctioned Reference Materials, various groups of political dissidents secretly compiled these documents and arranged for their distribution by quietly mailing them from such inauspicious places as the National Library in Peking. Clearly, the authors of these documents hoped to influence public opinion at home and abroad, perhaps in anticipation of or perhaps to instigate a political crisis after Chairman Mao's death. These documents arrived in the West shortly after the dates of their publication, which ranged between December 1975 and October 1977. Some relaxation of the customarily tight postal censorship in the populous megapolises of Peking and Shanghai must have occurred. This period was, after all, one of dramatic change from democratic centralism under the ailing and enfeebled Chairman Mao to the new triumvirate of Hua Kuo-feng, Yeh Chien-ying, and Teng Hsiao-p'ing.

Judging from the public statements of these same leaders, the new triumvirate presumably represents a dominant group and perhaps even encompasses a majority view across the complex political spectrum of the Communist party's 38 million members. Therefore, it is vitally important that as normalization between China and the United States occurs and China's leaders proceed with their Four Modernizations policy, we in the West remember that many shades of political opinion still exist among party leaders and throughout the party. Most of these views are no longer expressed. Yet in the four documents that I have translated here, these views are living and vibrant. Very possibly, the views expressed in these documents conceal a further range of political views.

THE ONLY GENUINE REVISIONIST

The first of these four documents, "Criticize and Overthrow the Biggest Revisionist Within the Party," was the only one translated here that was written before Mao's death, allegedly by the Central Extraordinary Committee of the Communist Party of China. Three thousand copies were reportedly published by the People's Press in Peking in December 1975, priced at RMB 0.08 yüan (approximately U.S. $0.05). These activists audaciously airmailed this pamphlet from Peking, supposedly through the Guozi Shudian (International Bookstore), marked P.O. Box 399, and bearing a postmark dated June 30, 1976. We cannot fully determine its authenticity, but certainly the stamps, paper, and printing are Chinese. In my opinion, this pamphlet originated from an ultraconservative faction within the Chinese Communist Party. Lo Chang-lung first organized the Central Extraordinary Committee, which represented the party's right wing, in Shanghai in early 1931. This faction may have remained alive and after 1949 recruited new members from sympathizers of the formerly senior-ranked Moscow-student group known as the Twenty-eight Bolsheviks and from some Russophile middle-echelon cadres and technocrats trained in the Soviet Union during the early years of the Sino-Soviet alliance (1949–1956). In any case, the conservative writers of this pamphlet label Mao Tse-tung the "biggest revisionist within the party." Yet they also oppose the "revisionist" policies and "social-imperialist" attitudes of the Russian communist leaders who came to power after Nikita Khrushchev launched his vitriolic attack on Stalin in 1956.

The document chastises Mao as a "genuine revisionist" and accuses him of "replacing truth by might." Consequently, many comrades were accused of committing the crime of revisionism in China between 1966 and 1975. The document further castigates Mao's famous dictum "the continuation of the class struggle for tens of thousands of years" as a leftist reflection of the hopelessness of the class struggle for the sake of restoring a feudal-slave society (Document I, p. 14; hereafter I, p. 14, according to the page number of the Chinese original). Mao is described as more leftist in "form" and more rightist in "substance" than Liu Shao-ch'i and Lin Piao (I, p. 15). The writers also criticize Mao's foreign policy for being "rightist." They contend that by inviting U.S. Presidents Nixon and Ford to China, Mao merely aped the coexistence diplomatic line of the Soviet Union (I, p. 19).

It is unlikely that Kuomintang agents forged this document for propaganda purposes. The pamphlet contains a rather unfavorable reference to Kuomintang rule: "Naturally, many among the masses have condemned our [socialist] reform of ownership of the means of production as [only] a change from the ownership of the Kuomintang and the landlord–rich peasant class to that of the Communist party" (I, p. 17). Moreover, I feel that the language of this publication often betrays ungrammatical and non-native use of words and expressions that would not have been written by native Chinese educated in China. In fact, the document could have been produced by Russian-trained dissidents with the collaboration of Soviet authorities. The Soviet Union maintains a large diplomatic and intelligence staff in China that can play a vital role in financing, assisting, and even backing the Moscow-educated Chinese comrades, who fell out of favor with Mao after the deterioration of the Sino-Soviet alliance. Some of the Russian-educated students, like Ch'en Shao-yü (who died in Moscow on March 27, 1974), may indeed have found refuge in the Soviet Union, but the majority of the Russophiles have no alternative but to remain in China. Significantly, this document credibly substantiates the existence of a strong, articulate, and determined pro-Soviet faction in China despite the polemical relations between the two communist countries.

Among the solecisms in this document are "ta-p'i-*ti*" (I, p. 1), "ti" ("target") as *suffix adjective*, rather than "ta-p'i-ti," "ti" ("earth") as *suffix adverb*; "fan-tung *liu-p'ai*" (I, p. 1), rather than "fan-tung *fen-tzu*"; "li-lun-yung-ch'i" (I, p. 3), rather than "li-lun-*shang-ti*-yung-ch'i"; "t'u-yang-*ping-chü*" (I, p. 4), rather than "t'u-yang-*chieh-ho*"; "wei-*hsieh*" (I, p. 8, "powerful agreement"), rather than "wei-*hsieh*" ("powerful coercion"); "Mao Tse-tung *ti*-i ch'üan-li tai-t'i chen-li" (I, p. 8), rather than "Mao Tse-tung i ch'üan-li tai-t'i chen-li"; "*hu*-li *hu-t'u*" (I, p. 10, "paste-inside paste-river's name"), rather than "*hu*-li *hu-t'u*" ("reckless-inside reckless-smear"); "*fen*" (I, p. 11, "divide"), rather than "*fen*" ("part"); "*chung*-kuo" (I, pp. 14 and 19, "Middle Kingdom"), rather than "*wo*-kuo" (our country); "Ch'in-shih-huang *shih*" (I, p. 18, "Ch'in-shih-huang style"), rather than "Ch'in-shih-huang"; "Mao Tse-tung *tzu-t'a*" (I, p. 20, "Mao Tse-tung since he"), rather than "Mao Tse-tung"; "chia-jen" (I, p. 20, "family members"), rather than "chia-t'ing" ("home"); "feng-chien-*hsing* she-hui" (I, p. 20), rather than "feng-chien she-hui"; and many others. Such errors are not normally made by native speakers of Chinese if they have been educated in China.

The authorship of this treatise may also be questioned on the grounds of its transliteration of Marx as "Ma-k'e-szu" ("horse-overcome-*thus*") throughout the document. Although the current standard Chinese characters for Marx are invariably "Ma-k'e-szu" ("horse-overcome-*think*"), many early Chinese communist leaders, as well as Comintern documents, adopted the transliteration "Ma-k'e-szu" (*thus*) during the 1930s when the Moscow-returned faction controlled the Communist Party of China. For example, Ch'ü Ch'iu-pai, the party's second secretary general, transliterated Marx in this manner throughout his last writing, "I and Marxism," before his execution on June 18, 1935. Since Engels and Stalin are customarily transliterated as "En-k'e-*szu*" (*thus*) and "*Szu*-ta-lin" (*thus*), a Russian-educated person might easily fall into the error of using the same character to transliterate Marx.

One of the most telling pieces of evidence attesting to the credibility of the first document lies in the date of its publication, December 1975. That year witnessed the convenings of the Second Plenum of the Tenth Central Committee of the Communist Party of China (January 8–10, 1975) and the Fourth National People's Congress (January 13–17), which elected Teng Hsiao-p'ing a vice chairman of the Central Committee and a member of the Standing Committee of the Politburo. During the first session of the Fourth National People's Congress on January 13, Premier Chou En-lai not only envisaged the attainment of the program of Four Modernizations before the end of this century, but also delivered a scathing attack on the Soviet Union: "The Soviet leading clique have betrayed Marxism-Leninism, and our debate with them on matters of principle will go on for a long time. . . . The Soviet leadership has taken a series of steps to worsen the relations between the two countries, conducted subversive activities against our country and even provoked armed conflicts on the border."[1] This document may well be the Chinese Russophiles' response to the Chinese Communist assault on the Soviet Union during the worsening polemic over Sino-Soviet relations.

THE LITTLE WHITE BOOK OF UNREVISED MAOIST DIPLOMACY

The second document, "Quotations from Chairman Mao on Revolutionary Diplomacy" (II, v, 124 pp.), appears to have been published by the People's Press in Peking in June 1977 at the price of RMB 0.66 yüan (approximately U.S. $0.40). A copy was airmailed to the United States allegedly by Guozi Shudian, P.O. Box 399, Peking, carrying a postmark of August 15, 1977. Apart from a "Publication Note" written in the name of the Committee for Editing and Publishing the *Works of Chairman Mao Tse-tung*, which is under the Central Committee of the Communist Party of China, this treatise contains 211 citations dated between November 6, 1938 and May 20, 1970. In fact, none of the selections quoted from volumes 1–5 of the *Selected Works of Mao Tse-tung* vary in wording from the texts in the official Chinese edition. In the "Publication Note," the committee directs vituperative criticism at both the United States and Russia: "The two superpowers, the Soviet Union and the United States, are currently the biggest international oppressors and exploiters, and the danger of a new world war emanates from these two hegemonies, especially from the social-imperialism of the Soviet Union" (II, p. 3). Significantly, however, seven of the thirteen sections (nos. 3 and 8–13) vilify the United States as the principal antagonist in Chairman Mao's revolutionary diplomacy. A large number of citations in the document predate the deterioration of Sino-Russian relations in the late 1950s and either praise or glorify the Soviet Union.

Under the heading "The Chinese Revolution Is Part of the World Revolution," section 1 dwells on the importance of forming an international united front against the capitalist world:

> Unite in a common struggle with those nations of the world that treat us as equals and unite with the peoples of all countries; this means to ally ourselves with the Soviet Union, with the people's democracies, and with the proletariat and the broad masses of the people in all other countries to form an international united front [II, pp. 6–7].

The section ends with a call:

> Our China not only is the political center of the world revolution, but must also become the military and technological center of the world revolution. We can give arms to the world revolution. We can do so openly, even if the arms are inscribed with [Chinese] characters. Yes, we will openly support revolutionaries and become the arsenal of the world revolution [II, p. 8].

The second section, "Learn From the Soviet Union," lists, among other things, reasons why China must learn from the Soviet Union: it was through the Soviets that the Chinese found Marxism (II, p. 9); a profound friendship has existed between the peoples of China and the Soviet Union since the Soviet government abrogated, after the October Revolution, the unequal treaties of the czarist era (II, p. 9); the Chinese can thus have access to the advanced Soviet experience, although they must carefully weigh the good and the bad. (II, pp. 10–11). The section concludes:

> No matter when, whether now or in the future, we of this generation and our offspring must learn from the Soviet Union and study the Soviet experience. . . . As for the bad people and bad things of the Soviet Union, as well as the revisionists of the Soviet Union, we should treat them as teachers by negative example from whom we shall draw our lessons [II, pp. 14–15].

According to section 3, "The Two Camps," the world is divided into two opposing fronts: imperialism, which is the front oppressing the people, and socialism, which is the front resisting this oppression (II, p. 17).

Neutrality between the two camps is merely a deception (II, p. 18). "If we stand between the Soviet Union and the United States, it looks very good and independent but is not so in reality. Since the United States is unreliable, it will give you something but not very much. How could the United States completely feed [all of] us?" (II, p. 20). Chairman Mao's prophetic views on the policy of "leaning to one side" are intriguing:

> In the light of the experiences accumulated in these 40 years [of Sun Yat-sen's revolution, 1885–1925] and these 28 years [of the Chinese Communist revolution, 1921–1949], all Chinese without exception must lean either to the side of imperialism or to the side of socialism. Sitting on the fence will not do, nor is there a third road [II, pp. 21–22].

Chairman Mao's preference is unambiguous:

> Who designed and equipped so many important factories for us? Was it the United States? Or Britain? No, neither the one nor the other. Only the Soviet Union was willing to do so because it is a socialist country and our ally. In addition to the Soviet Union, the fraternal countries in East Europe have also given us some assistance [II, p. 22].

The section sums up:

> We are united with all Marxist-Leninists, all revolutionary comrades, and the entire people, and never with the anticommunists and antipeople imperialists or the reactionaries in various countries. If possible, we shall establish diplomatic relations with these people and seek peaceful coexistence on the basis of the five principles [II, p. 26].[2]

Labeled "The Two Roads," the fourth section emphasizes the importance of pursuing the communist, as opposed to the capitalist, road. The Chinese must firmly reject and criticize all decadent bourgeois systems, ideologies, and foreign ways of life. But this rule should not prevent China from learning advanced science and technology and the scientific aspects of enterprise management from the capitalist countries (II, p. 29). Moreover, the Chinese wish to extinguish capitalism and turn the bourgeoisie into a relic of history (II, p. 32). "We must unite," the section exhorts, "with the Soviet Union, the fraternal parties, and the parties from 87 countries, no matter what names they have called us"

(II, p. 32). "In Sino-Soviet relations," it concludes, "bickering always happens. Do not imagine that there can be no bickering in the world. Marxism is bickering-ism, for there are always contradictions" (II, p. 36).

Section 5, "The Two Lines" (that is, the revisionist and Marxist lines), reprimands both dogmatism and revisionism for being anti-Marxist. Revisionism or rightist opportunism is, however, condemned as the more dangerous trend of thought (II, p. 38). "Although the party and state leadership of the Soviet Union," it sums up, "is now usurped by revisionists, I [Mao] wish to persuade you comrades to believe firmly that the majority of the Soviet Union's masses and party members, as well as cadres, are good and want to wage revolution. This revisionist rule will not last long" (II, p. 47).

Entitled "Nationalism," the sixth section asserts that no matter what classes, parties, or individuals in an oppressed nation join a nationalist revolution, and no matter whether they themselves are conscious of or understand the point, so long as they oppose imperialism, their revolution becomes part of the proletarian-socialist world revolution and they become its allies (II, p. 49). "But these groups cannot include the reactionary national bourgeoisie like Nehru or reactionary bourgeois intellectuals, such as the Japanese communist renegade Kanga Shōjirō who advocates the theory of organizational reform, along with six or seven other persons" (II, p. 53).

Section 7, "Imperialism," identifies the United States as the arch villain: "With the exception of Australia, the United States now wants to infringe on the other four of the five continents" (II, p. 58). "The imperialists are really dispirited," the section concludes, "They are decadent, confused, full of contradictions, and badly divided. They are ill at ease, and their good days are in the past" (II, p. 63).

The eighth section is entitled "War and Peace." The reactionary forces of the world have already prepared for a third world war, this section asserts, but they are greatly outnumbered by the democratic forces, which are forging ahead and can certainly overcome the danger of war (II, p. 64). "The danger of a world war," it is pointed out here (and repeated in Section 13 [II, p. 118]), "and the threat to China come mainly from U.S. warmongers. They have occupied our Taiwan and the Taiwan Strait and are contemplating an atomic war. We have two principles: (1) we do not want war; and (2) we will strike back resolutely if invaded" (II, p. 67). As another citation stresses, war is a means of class conflicts. Only through war can classes be extinguished; only after the extinction of classes can war be permanently eliminated (II, p. 72). "China wants peace," the section sums up succinctly. "Whoever advocates peace has our support. We are not in favor of war. But we support the wars of oppressed peoples against imperialism" (II, p. 76).

Under the title, "Oppose the Policies of Aggression and War," section 9 quotes Mao Tse-tung's statement that the American people and the people of all countries menaced by U.S. aggression must unite and struggle against the attacks of the U.S. reactionaries and their running dogs. Only by victory in this struggle can a third world war be avoided; otherwise, it is inevitable (II, p. 82). The section concludes:

> People of all countries in the socialist camp, unite; people of all countries in Asia, Africa, and Latin America, unite; people of all continents in the whole world, unite; all peace-loving countries, unite; all those countries that have been invaded, controlled, suffered intervention, and been maltreated by the United States, unite. [We] must form the broadest [possible] united front, oppose the warmongering and aggressive policies of U.S. imperialism, and safeguard world peace [II, p. 85].

The tenth section, "Resisting U.S. Aggression and Aiding Korea," attributes China's success to leadership and popular support: "Leadership is one factor; nothing can succeed without correct leadership. But we won mainly because ours was a people's war; the whole nation supported it, and the peoples of China and Korea fought shoulder to shoulder" (II, p. 88). As for China's basic policy toward imperialist aggression:

> Imperialism calls us "aggressors" and "bellicose elements." In a certain way, this is correct because of our support of Castro, Ben Bella, and the war of the people of South Vietnam against the United States. Moreover, in 1950–1953, the United States invaded Korea, and we supported the war of the Korean people against U.S. imperialism. This policy of ours has been openly declared, and we shall never give it up. We must support the war of the people of all countries against imperialism. If we don't, we shall be committing a mistake and not be communists [II, p. 95].

Section 11, "The Third World," contains the only reference critical of the preeminent Russian revolutionary leader:

> Lenin said: "The more backward the country, the more difficult is its tran-

sition from capitalism to socialism." This statement now seems incorrect. In reality, the more backward the economy, the easier is its transition from capitalism to socialism, not the more difficult. The poorer the people, the more revolutionary they are [II, p. 99].

In another quotation, Chairman Mao is cited as alerting his followers to the danger of being swayed by China's own propaganda:

The goal of the North Atlantic Treaty Organization is to attack nationalism and indigenous communism in its member states (concentrating on attacking the intermediate zone—Asia, Africa, and Latin America). It has been defensive toward the socialist camp, except for the Hungarian incident. But in [our] propaganda we say on the contrary that its purpose is to launch an attack [on socialism]. Do not be misled by our own propaganda [II, p. 105].

The twelfth section, "American Imperialism Is a Paper Tiger," elaborates on this notable dictum:

When we say American imperialism is a paper tiger, we are speaking in terms of strategy. Regarding it as a whole, we must belittle it. But regarding each part, we must take it seriously. It has claws and fangs, and we must destroy it piecemeal. . . . If we deal with it earnestly step by step, we will certainly succeed in the end. . . . Tactically, we must take it seriously [II, p. 110].

With respect to atom and hydrogen bombs, the section concludes: "Imperialism brandishes its atom bombs and its hydrogen bombs to scare us, but they don't frighten us either. The world is so constituted that there is always one thing to conquer another. When one thing is used in an attack, there is bound to be another thing to conquer it" (II, p. 117).

The final section, "The People's War," reads:

Our national defense will be consolidated, and no imperialists will ever again be allowed to invade our land. Our people's armed forces must be maintained and developed on the foundation of the heroic and steeled People's Liberation Army. We will have not only a powerful army but also a powerful air force and a powerful navy [II, p. 119].

As if to underscore the exorbitant cost of the people's war in terms of
Chinese suffering and lives, the section cites Chairman Mao's sanguine
and sanguinary assessment:

> If an enemy breaks in, we can fight our way out. Generally speaking, we
> are prepared to fight, to wage battles intrepidly, and to deal with atom
> bombs coolly. Fear not. The worst that can happen is universal confusion
> and the death of some. Everyone must die, whether standing up or lying
> down. Carry on if alive, and half our people will survive even if the other
> half die [II, p. 123].

It is significant that this document was supposedly published in June
1977 in Peking, eight months after the purge of the Gang of Four (October 6, 1976) but one month before the opening of the Third Plenum
(July 16–21, 1977) of the Tenth Central Committee. This plenum not
only adopted the resolution confirming the appointment of Hua Kuo-
feng as chairman of the Central Committee and its Military Commission
(which had first been approved by the Politburo on October 7, 1976, in
accordance with the arrangements allegedly made by Chairman Mao
before his death on September 9), but also passed the resolution restoring Teng Hsiao-p'ing to all his posts.[3] This period (October 6, 1976–
July 21, 1977) was one of an unsettling leadership crisis, in which some
fundamental domestic and foreign policy issues had to be resolved.
Given these circumstances, this document was most likely printed by
some conservative elements as an instrument or a basis for initiating
discussion within the rank and file of the upper hierarchy, if not the
party membership, of Chairman Mao's supposed views on China's so-
called revolutionary diplomacy. Needless to say, the opinions in these
quotations from Mao, which cast a favorable light on the Russians, are
not shared by the emerging leadership headed by Chairman Hua Kuo-
feng. Therefore, this document, although compiled by the same official
committee that edited and published volume 5 of the *Selected Works of
Mao Tse-tung*, has never been officially distributed outside China. Chairman Mao's kind words on the Soviet Union to some extent caused the
long delay until April 1977 in the publication of volume 5 of the *Selected
Works of Mao Tse-tung*; volume 4 was published in September 1960. (In-
cidentally, Mao Tse-tung's sobering statement that half of China's population would die in the event of atomic war may account for the current
Four Modernizations program, which includes the modernization of
national defense.)

OPPOSITION TO RIGHTIST CAPITULATIONISM

Under the title "Pursuing the Proletarian Revolutionary Line or the Rightist Capitulationist Line?" (III, 30 pp.), the third document was allegedly issued by the Shanghai Municipal Committee of the Communist Youth League on June 30, 1977, and published in a run of 200,000 copies by the People's Press in Shanghai in the same month at RMB 0.14 yüan (approximately U.S. $0.08). One copy was airmailed to this country apparently by the International Exchange Section of the National Library in Peking on July 20, 1977.

This pamphlet appears to have been compiled by remnant sympathizers of the Gang of Four. It is hardly surprising that the pamphlet was printed in Shanghai, the former bulwark of the Gang, and issued by the Communist Youth League, whose leadership had been seized by the Gang after its organizational activities were seriously disrupted by thousands of rampaging Red Guards during the Cultural Revolution. Thus, the very recent national congress of the Communist Youth League (the tenth) belatedly took place on October 16–26, 1978, in Peking, despite the fact that its Ninth National Congress (attended by Mao Tse-tung) occurred in 1964.

As the *Peking Review* puts it:

Lin Piao and the "Gang of Four" once deceived many innocent young people by waving "revolutionary" flags. These political swindlers dismembered, trampled on, and distorted Marxism/Leninism/Mao Tse-tung Thought, and their advocacy of extremely reactionary pragmatism and obscurantism mentally shackled some young people for a long time or infected them with nihilist tendencies towards revolutionary theory. . . . In some places anarchism and unsavoury bourgeois trends were rife and gravely impaired the healthy growth of our young people.[4]

Furthermore, the Gang's control of Shanghai seemed to continue after Chairman Mao's death on September 9, 1976:

After the Party Central Committee headed by Chairman Hua had crushed the "Gang of Four," a few trusted followers of the gang in Shanghai, though already knowing this through a secret channel, ordered local newspapers to continue publishing articles on the theme, "act according to the principles laid down," and the local radio stations to keep broadcasting the song, "Act Forever According to the Principles Laid Down." All this was part of their effort to stage a counter-revolutionary armed rebellion.[5]

In another article in the *Peking Review*:

When Chairman Mao was seriously ill and after he passed away, they [the Gang] quickened the pace to usurp Party and state power. Without authorization, they turned industrial plants in Shanghai making non-military products into arsenals and hastily issued huge quantities of arms and ammunition to the members of the people's militia, and again without authorization, ordered troop movements, set up clandestine command centres, compiled codes for use in secret communications, and conspired to launch a counter-revolutionary armed rebellion. They clamoured that they were ready to engage the Party Central Committee headed by Chairman Hua in a "bloody war" and "fight to the finish."[6]

Undoubtedly the document takes decided issue with current Chinese leaders on the basis of the "Message to the Whole Party, the Whole Army, and the People of All Nationalities Throughout the Country," which was issued by the Central Committee of the Communist Party of China, the Standing Committee of the National People's Congress, the State Council, and the Military Commission on September 9, 1976.[7] This message calls on the party, the army, and all nationalities in the country to turn their grief over Mao's death into strength to fulfill six tasks: (1) persisting in taking the class struggle as the key link [of the revolution]; (2) strengthening the unified leadership; (3) consolidating the great unity of the people of all nationalities, deepening the criticism of Teng Hsiao-p'ing, and continuing the struggle to repulse the rightist reversal of [party] verdicts; (4) resolutely implementing Chairman Mao's line in army building; (5) continuing to carry out resolutely Chairman Mao's revolutionary line and policies in foreign affairs; and (6) assiduously studying Marxism-Leninism–Mao Tse-tung Thought. But, the document charges, present leaders have at the very least failed to carry on the cause left behind by Chairman Mao in the first three tasks.

Regarding the first accusation, on the subject of "taking the class struggle as the key link," the document states: "At present, the small counterrevolutionary, double-faced clique within the party, with Hua Kuo-feng in control of the party's Central Committee, continuously pays lip service to the slogan of taking the class struggle as the key link. . . . but inwardly they merely take Teng Hsiao-p'ing's 'three directives as the key link' " (III, p. 4).[8] The document continues:

> The phrases used by Hua Kuo-feng and company—"taking the key link to govern the country," "great order to prevail soon," and "pushing the national economy forward"—are in essence carbon copies of Teng Hsiao-p'ing's so-called "promoting stability and unity" and "pushing the national economy forward." . . . This aptly reveals the similarity of their [Hua and company's] reactionary viewpoint to that previously declared by Teng Hsiao-p'ing and company in the so-called "On the General Program for All Work of the Whole Party and the Whole Country" and demonstrates their persistence in the revisionist "theory of sole reliance on productive force" [III, pp. 4–5].[9]

With respect to the second task, strengthening the party's unified leadership and persevering in maintaining the party's unity and solidarity, the document alleges that within a month after Chairman Mao's death, a serious schism occurred within the party. The leading comrades, Wang Hung-wen, Chang Chün-chiao, Chiang Ch'ing, and Yao Wen-yüan of the party's Central Committee, were incarcerated by the small, intraparty, counterrevolutionary, double-faced clique led by Hua Kuo-feng. The document then remonstrates:

> On May 3, 1975, at a meeting of the Central Committee Politburo, Chairman Mao reiterated the basic principle of the "three do's and three don'ts." These were aimed at the small intraparty clique of unrepentant capitalist roaders led by Teng Hsiao-p'ing, who, after the Fourth People's Congress [January 13–17, 1975], conspired to restore the reactionary essence of capitalism on the pretext of carrying out the Four Modernizations over the next 25 years. Chairman Mao warned them: "Do practice Marxism; don't practice revisionism. Do unite; don't split. Do be open and aboveboard; don't intrigue and conspire" [III, p. 6].

But who would have thought, the document exclaims, that the three do's and three don'ts used by Chairman Mao to refer to the conspiracy to restore capitalism by Teng Hsiao-p'ing and company would be twisted by Hua Kuo-feng and company to become Mao's criticism of Wang, Chang, Chiang, and Yao? (III, p. 7). It is especially serious, according to the document, that after incarcerating Wang, Chang, Chiang, and

Yao [reportedly on October 6, 1976], the present leaders further attacked all those good, young comrades, most of whom had entered the party only since the Cultural Revolution and constituted more than one-third of the total membership of the party. As a result of Hua and company's practice of revisionism, schism, and conspiratorial trickery and their destruction of party unity and solidarity, the party and country have once again been led into the serious crisis of a great schism and a leap backward (III, p. 10).

Concerning the third accusation and referring to the need for "consolidating the great unity of the people of all nationalities, deepening the criticism of Teng Hsiao-p'ing, and continuing the struggle to repulse the rightist reversal of verdicts," the document alleges that current leaders have turned criticism of Teng Hsiao-p'ing on its head:

> In recent months, an almost incredible event has occurred. Hua Kuo-feng and company have gone so far as to invoke repeatedly in their propaganda the Confucian saying, "Hear one's words and judge one by his deeds," that Teng Hsiao-p'ing quoted on October 29, 1975, during a speech before visiting German Federal Republic Chancellor Helmut Schmidt and his wife.[10]

The document continues: "This incident truly reveals that Hua Kuo-feng and company are basically not criticizing but praising Teng. At the same time, this incident also shows that these fellows do not criticize Confucius, but really behave in a reactionary way of venerating Confucius" (III, pp. 12–13). On the convening of the Second National Conference on Learning from Tachai in Agriculture (December 10–27, 1976) and the National Conference on Learning from Taching in Industry (April 20–May 13, 1977) under the auspices of current leaders, the document states: "Their real objectives were to implement on an extensive basis the reversal of verdicts and the restoration [of capitalism]" (III, p. 15). The document sums up:

> After the party's Central Committee was taken over by the small counter-revolutionary, intraparty, double-faced clique led by Hua Kuo-feng, who with open mouth has screamed the Thought of Mao Tse-tung but has committed criminal acts behind everyone's back against the party, socialism, and the Thought of Mao Tse-tung, our party now no longer follows the proletarian revolutionary line. It is following the rightist, capitulationist line [III, p. 19].

Finally, for the sake of enhancing its own credibility with the populace, the document condemns the excesses of the Gang of Four: "During the course of the Great Cultural Revolution, when Wang Hung-wen, Chang Chün-chiao, Chiang Ch'ing, and Yao Wen-yüan rose up brazenly to heaven, haughtily treading on everyone's rights and isolating themselves from the masses, they certainly had no sufficient cause for success but ample grounds for disaster." In conclusion, the document calls on all young Communist party and Communist Youth League members to "direct the spearhead of struggle against Hua Kuo-feng and company and sweep away into the garbage bin of history all monsters and demons of any size who have betrayed the party and the country" (III, pp. 19–20).

THE EXTREME RADICALS' ATTACK

The fourth document, "Pledge to Carry Out the Proletarian Revolution to the End" (IV, 12 pp.), was supposedly written by the Great Criticism Section of the Kiangsi Communist Labor University of the Communist Party of China on October 20, 1977, and published by the Kiangsi People's Press. Several copies were airmailed under different names from Shanghai on November 5, 1977, to the United States. Interestingly enough, the following covering letter *in English* was enclosed with each copy:

Dear Sir:

While Hua Kuo-feng's regime of China [*sic*] is on the upswing to expose and criticize the "GANG OF FOUR" throughout China, we have found a pamphlet, entitled "PLEDGE TO CARRY OUT THE PROLETARIAN REVOLUTION TO THE END,"[11] signed by the "Chiangshi [Kiangsi] Communist Labour University." Being circulated secretly among people of all strata, the pamphlet lays a lot of blame on the political systems [*sic*] under Hua's leadership and wins favourable echoes from the masses.

From the enclosed pamphlet, you'll perceive the lofty ideal and the unremitting spirit held by the Chinese proletariat class for the construction of communism as well as the prospect of a new China.

Our best wishes.

Sincerely yours,
[Signed in different Chinese names]

The Gang of Four not only brought turmoil to Shanghai and neigh-
boring cities in Kiangsu during the Cultural Revolution but also to other
provinces, including Kiangsi. For example, the *Peking Review* com-
mented of the Gang's seizure of power in Kiangsi: "The gang was over-
joyed early last year [1976] when they received an anonymous letter
from Kiangsi Province viciously attacking the provincial Party committee.
Chiang Ch'ing herself arranged to find out the writer of the letter
and incited him to stir up trouble in Kiangsi."[12] The Kiangsi Communist
Labor University, China's oldest "half-work and half-study" new-style
educational institution, was founded at Nanchang on August 1, 1958,
during the Great Leap Forward, with thirty subcampuses throughout
Kiangsi.[13] During the Cultural Revolution, the university expanded to
include one main campus and 132 subcampuses, with nearly 50,000
students.[14] Judging by its organization, curriculum, and student body,
the university ranks among China's most radical, revolutionary, and
proletarian-conscious institutions.[15] It is highly possible that by October
1977 this university had become a stronghold of the extreme leftist followers of the Gang of Four.

The document singles out present leaders as its prime target for assault: "The great revolutionary teacher, Chairman Mao, wisely predicted before passing away that a handful of careerists and conspirators
would definitely engage in an anticommunist, rightist coup d'etat after
his death" (IV, p. 1). Within a month after Chairman Mao's death on
September 9, 1976, the document points out, the new leaders arrested
the Gang of Four, an act that nullified the principles and policies of the
Cultural Revolution (IV, p. 2).

Although the dismissal of Teng Hsiao-p'ing was endorsed by Mao
and the Politburo, the document charges, Hua Kuo-feng and his henchmen have now pronounced that Mao's directive on this subject was
forged.[16] Eventually, the document continues, all Chairman Mao's directives will be declared forgeries except the memorandum proclaiming,
"With you in charge, I am at ease," a statement that the document alleges
was forged by the current leaders.[17]

In addition, the document condemns the present leaders' efforts to
establish "commissions for inspecting discipline" at all levels, likening
these efforts to Liu Shao-ch'i's attempt to effect "monolithic organizational control" of the party and Lin Piao's use of "assaulting a great mass
and protecting a small handful" of people as a means of seizing and
retaining power (IV, p. 8).[18] Finally, the document sums up:

At present, they [the current leaders] have already reached the height of their craze, and the eleventh struggle about the [correct] line of our party is also the struggle of our whole party, our whole army, and the people of all nationalities throughout the country against the handful of remnants of capitalist roaders, consisting of Hua [Kuo-feng], Yeh [Chien-ying], Teng [Hsiao-p'ing], Li [Hsien-nien], and Wang [Tung-hsing]. This must be carried out by us, who are of a younger generation and dare to turn back the tide with even greater unity and determination. . . .

We pledge to carry out the Chinese proletarian revolution to the end and to create a beautiful tomorrow from our labors [IV, pp. 11–12].

These are the parting salvos of the surviving diehards from the extreme radical sector of the party, formerly led by the Gang of Four.

It is difficult to understand how these polemical *samizdat* documents could have been compiled in and sent out of the People's Republic of China. Over the years we have been led to believe that the vast, sophisticated, and ingenious Chinese population has been successfully transformed under the aegis of the monolithic Communist Party of China headed by the supreme helmsman Chairman Mao Tse-tung into a nation of faceless "blue ants" dedicated to the realization of the proletarian revolution in that country, if not in the third world. Our limited access to China has indeed bred numerous instances of confusion, misunderstanding, and even myth. Yet with the process of normalization under way, we have now come to form a new image of the ancient Middle Kingdom. Not only has Vice-Premier Teng Hsiao-p'ing been selected by a popular newsmagazine as "Man of the Year"[19] and welcomed by President Jimmy Carter at the White House during his state visit between January 28 and February 5, 1979, but the streets of Peking have also witnessed quite a few posters advocating "democracy" and even appealing to President Carter to intervene in China on behalf of "human rights." A few years ago, who would have thought we would see Chinese wall posters in Peking protesting the invasion of Vietnam in early 1979?[20]

Some of these wall posters are known to have been surreptitiously published in Peking and elsewhere since late 1978 in the so-called *min-pan k'an-wu* (people's magazines), such as *Pei-ching-chih-ch'un* (The Spring of Peking), *Min-chu yü shih-tai* (Democracy and the Times), *Ch'iu-shih pao* (The Quest for Truth), *Chung-kuo jen-ch'üan* (Chinese Human Rights), *T'an-so* (Search and Demand), *Hsin t'ien-ti* (New Heaven and Earth), *Ssu-*

wu lun-t'an (April Fifth Forum), *Ch'i-meng* (Awakening), *Chin-t'ien* (To-day), *Ch'ün-chung ts'an-k'ao tzu-liao* (Masses Reference Materials), and the like. Appearing irregularly in the streets, these underground journals are vehemently critical of the government's stand on political freedom, economic reforms, and ideological control.

In the words of a "Reporter's Commentary" in *Pei-ching-chih-ch'un:*

> With a view to searching and demanding the truth and to exercising the democratic rights stipulated in the constitution [adopted on March 1, 1978, at the first session of the Fifth National People's Congress], a number of courageous young people are personally determined to test the validity of the law by operating a few magazines with their own resources. . . . The locations of the individual editorial departments cannot easily be fixed, for most of them are "editorial departments in exile." The braver ones have published their home addresses so that readers may send in manuscripts and communications, and the more timid ones can only resort to other means because the plainclothes police may have already set their "sharp" eyes on [them] in the dark [no. 2, January 27, 1979, p. 4].

Many of these magazines were shut down and their operators arrested during the spring of 1979, owing to their scathing attacks on the government and its top leaders, including Chairman Hua Kuo-feng and Vice-Premier Teng Hsiao-p'ing.

Since these people's magazines, which have emerged mostly since late 1978, are similar to dissident literature in content, they were without doubt inspired by the *samizdat* documents that preceded them between December 1975 and October 1977. It must also be stressed that the *samizdat* documents appear to have more significance than the people's magazines because the former dwell on the burning issues of the Chinese socialist revolution, while the latter deal with a tantalizing hodgepodge of public protest and personal complaints. The former are all typeset, which seems to signify a far more powerful or numerous grouping of persons behind them than the latter, which are all mimeographed—perhaps by a handful of enterprising individuals. The people's magazines are of tremendous interest to both scholar and nonscholar alike in the West, but I feel that they must be studied and analyzed separately, owing to their numbers.

Given the almost incredible nature of developments during the current transitional period, I believe that the four documents translated here are authentic. Throughout Chinese history, the tradition of engaging in unflinching dissent with "wrongful" authorities has always been deep-rooted. Celebrated examples of recent times include the Hundred Flowers campaign (1956), P'eng Te-huai (1959), Wu Han (1965), Li I-che (1974), and many others.[21] What emanates from these four documents is that Chinese political thought remains lively, innovative, and responsive to the basic needs of a changing society, even within the confines of Marxism-Leninism and the Thought of Mao Tsetung.

Documents

Criticize and Overthrow the Biggest Revisionist Within the Party

(The People's Press, Peking, December 29, 1975)

DOCUMENT ONE

諫 Comrades in the whole party and the whole army:

During the decade since the Eleventh Plenum [1966] of the party's Eighth Central Committee, many party comrades who are loyal to Marxism are considered to have committed the error of "revisionism" either in theory or in practice. Of particular seriousness is that these are not individual, adventitious cases of persons committing errors. Such cases have appeared frequently and in great numbers. Should Marxism therefore be revised? Why have so many comrades committed the "revisionist" mistake? Now is the time to adopt the ideological weapon of Marxism and earnestly clarify this problem.

First, we must emphasize that we wish to do so not because we side with the late-1890s reactionaries who were not only hostile to Marxism, but also acted contrary to dialectical materialism under the banners of "reinvestigating" and "revising" the philosophical basis of Marxism. Nor are we in agreement with those unrealistic, dogmatic activities that are not based on reality and totally separate textbook theories from revolutionary practices. At the same time, we firmly oppose those who have on the pretext of developing Marxism guided this science backward from either the leftist or the rightist direction. Further, we firmly oppose those few careerists and conspirators within the party who have utilized anti-"revisionism" as a camouflage for maintaining their vested interests, as well as for securing more power, and for plotting unrelentingly against the large number of comrades who remain loyal to Marxism. We affirm that we are completely and firmly grounded on developing Marxism to analyze the current problem.

We shall first discuss the question whether Marxism should be revised; this is the fundamental problem that needs clarifying now. Moreover, it is inappropriate for only a few [of us] to undertake this clarification. We must let comrades in the whole party and the whole army know and let the revolutionary people in the whole nation know.

In order to clarify the problem whether Marxism should indeed be revised, let us quote a paragraph from Lenin:

> We shall never regard Marxist theories as immutable and sacrosanct. On the contrary, we believe that they only lay the foundation for a kind of science. If socialists do not wish to lag behind the reality of life, they should promote the advancement of this science in every respect (*Complete Works of Lenin*, 4: 187).

Because of this viewpoint, Lenin did not enslave himself to the [exact] words, phrases, and sentences of Marxism. Under the new conditions of class struggle between the bourgeoisie and the proletariat, he courageously applied the appropriate theories and relinquished outdated, particular principles and conclusions in Marxism, replacing them with new principles and conclusions that became the new historical circumstances, thus making substantial revisions of Marxism.

As for the "Thought of Mao Tse-tung," Mao Tse-tung and his advocates have proclaimed that Mao Tse-tung has applied his supreme theoretical accomplishments and his greatest theoretical courage and daringly made fearless, theoretical creations that relinquished outdated, particular principles and conclusions in Marxism that do not accord with concrete conditions in China, replacing them with new principles and conclusions that have become the new Chinese historical circumstances. In essence, however, there is no doubt that the "Thought of Mao Tse-tung" combines indigenous and foreign ideas and substantially revises both Marxism and Leninism.

Therefore, if revising Marxism-Leninism is revisionism, then the "Thought of Mao Tse-tung" is a [kind of] revisionism of Marxism-Leninism and Mao Tse-tung is himself a genuine revisionist.

Truth develops from its struggle with falsehood. Marxism is a science concerned with the laws of natural and social developments, a science concerned with the revolution of the oppressed and exploited masses, and a science concerned with the worldwide victory of socialism. This science cannot be slowed. At the same time, Marxism is also the most vital and world-reforming revolutionary teaching; it is totally irreconcilable with dogmatism and stereotyped party writing. From its inception, in order to continue to forge ahead, Marxism has had to absorb new experience and knowledge so that it could enrich itself as it developed. Its individual formulas and conclusions must be modified over time and replaced by new formulas and conclusions commensurate with new historical missions. Thus, we can reach a simple conclusion: Revisions of Marxism are necessary if Marxism is found to be wrong in practice; further revisions can be made if the situation is still incorrect. In fact, this science is forever developing and improving.

On the basis of the above analysis, we are aware that Marxism is not immutable; it not only can but also should be revised in order to accord with new historical circumstances. This has been demonstrated by Lenin and Mao Tse-tung. At the current stage, in order to enable all comrades in the whole party and the whole army to clarify this problem, let us hope that [our] comrades will frequently discuss this opinion of ours.

Now we shall further analyze another question, namely, that of why so many comrades have during the recent decade committed the mistake of "revisionism." This is an important problem that concerns the individual future of comrades in the whole party and the whole army, as well as the success or failure of the socialist revolutionary enterprise of our party. It is what we must also clarify.

In fact, all aspects of socialism can be thoroughly discussed. Criticizing erroneous opinions and supporting correct opinions are both essential. "Odd doctrines and heretical sayings" are not at all frightening, but they have been the pretexts for the inevitable downfall of many comrades who, although loyal to Marxism, have been considered "revisionist," and whose so-called "revisionism" is further considered to have violated the heavenly commandment [*sic*]. This is because might has been substituted for truth throughout the party since Mao Tse-tung usurped the authority of the party's Central Committee [in 1945].

By replacing truth by might, Marxism does not thereby become immutable and sacrosanct. Yet the Thought of Mao Tse-tung is regarded as immutable and sacrosanct. Although Marxism can be revised [by Mao] on various pretexts, we must "closely follow the great leader Chairman Mao," "closely follow the great Thought of Mao Tse-tung," "closely follow the proletarian revolutionary line of Chairman Mao," and "closely

follow the proletarian headquarters led by Mao Tse-tung." Whether he
is right or wrong, we have to follow suit. If anyone dares to violate this
principle, it is unforgivable "revisionism," and he must be seized, dragged
down, trodden on, and never be allowed to make the slightest twitch.

Since might has been substituted for truth, all sayings of Mao Tse-
tung, whether the ravings of a high fever or a nightmare, are "absolute
decrees," "supreme directives," to be "steadfastly carried out" and "persistently complied with." No dissent is permitted. Any expression of
opinion is tantamount to "dabbling in bourgeois restorationism" and to
"dabbling in revisionism." According to Mao Tse-tung's views, Ch'in
Shih-huang's [Chinese emperor, 221–209 B.C.] mass execution of people
who might vilify him was a mere trifle compared with the doings of
"such prominent personages as are seen during current [Mao's] times."

Of particular seriousness is that since Mao Tse-tung has replaced
truth by might, everything has depended on the whims of his own personal power because "the Big Daddy [Mao] is the foremost under
Heaven." In order to maintain his vested interests, as well as to secure
even more power, he has regarded all revolutionary comrades who
steadfastly adhere to principles and remain loyal to Marxism as public
enemies and has attacked them without mercy, not even excepting his
own "dear comrades" and "successors."

We may recall that Liu Shao-ch'i was always Mao Tse-tung's most val-
ued assistant in maintaining Mao's vested interests, as well as in securing
him more power after the Tsun-i Conference of January 1935; Mao
Tse-tung was glorified during the party's Seventh National Congress in
1945 as a "talented and creative Marxist" by none other than Liu Shao-
ch'i. At that Congress, none other than Liu Shao-ch'i affirmed for the
first time that the Thought of Mao Tse-tung was the guiding ideology
for our whole party and the compass for the party's various endeavors.
Later during the various rectification movements, Mao Tse-tung was
wholeheartedly supported by none other than Liu Shao-ch'i. But after
Liu Shao-ch'i succeeded Mao Tse-tung as chief [chairman] of state,
which damaged Mao Tse-tung's vested powers, Liu Shao-ch'i was in-
stantly transformed from Mao Tse-tung's successor to "the biggest revisionist within the party," who had to be overthrown.

Another prime example is Lin Piao. Lin Piao was dragged into part-
nership when Mao Tse-tung sought to recoup his lost powers from Liu
Shao-ch'i. Lin Piao may be said to have glorified the Thought of Mao
Tse-tung twice as much as Liu Shao-ch'i did and to have carried out the

Thought of Mao Tse-tung more thoroughly. All the vocabulary of glor-
ification and flattery—"talented," "creative," "authoritative," "supreme,"
"greatest," "exciting," "absolute," "steadfast," and "study Chairman Mao's
books, listen to Chairman Mao's words, act according to Chairman Mao's
directives, serve as a good fighter of Chairman Mao"—was put to use.
Lin Piao's actions during the Great Cultural Revolution in recouping
powers from Liu Shao-ch'i and company on behalf of Mao Tse-tung
were so especially sanguinary that the skies became dizzy, the earth dark-
ened, the "ghosts" cried, and the "gods" wailed. But when Mao Tse-tung
felt that Lin Piao was gradually encroaching on his vested powers, Lin
Piao was again transformed—from "Chairman Mao's dear comrade . . .
legal successor" to one of "Liu Shao-ch'i's ilk."

As a result of Mao Tse-tung's replacing of truth by might, everything
depends on the whims of power. Relevant examples are too numerous
to be listed. Comrade Teng To has stated that Mao Tse-tung "becomes
happy or angry without cause" and "says things without reason." Comrade Ch'en I has stated that Mao Tse-tung "demolishes bridges after
crossing them." These allegations are certainly not without foundation.
Since "forgiving the enemy is tantamount to inflicting damage on one-
self," dealing with "revisionism" is certainly a matter of cutting "weeds"
and digging up their roots. Thus, many good comrades who merely had
incidental relations with Liu Shao-ch'i or Lin Piao were regarded as having committed the error of "revisionism." Under the conditions of ever
deepening and developing struggles, they were seized one after the
other, then beheaded if found "culpable," or else imprisoned if found
"culpable," or else inducted into the May 7th Cadre School if found
"culpable." This is the real reason that during the decade since the Eleventh Plenum of the party's Eighth Central Committee, so many comrades have been accused of committing the mistake of "revisionism."

No one will deny that during recent years as a result of replacing
truth with might, replacing objectivity with subjectivity, replacing scientific analysis with hallucination, Mao Tse-tung has made numerous
erroneous revisions within the party with respect to the development of
Marxism, causing severe destruction of the socialist revolutionary enterprise that had increasingly been prospering and flourishing since the
liberation of the entire nation. Every comrade in the whole party and
the whole army has witnessed the serious consequences of the general
line, the Great Leap Forward, and the people's communes in 1958, as
well as those of the Great Cultural Revolution in 1966.[1] Liu Shao-ch'i

and Lin Piao, in pursuing the erroneous revisionist line against Marxism because of their craving for more power, were but Mao Tse-tung's flatterers and promoters. Each was subsequently overthrown and labeled as wearing the revisionist cap of opportunism in power struggles. The biggest revisionist in the party, who has truly made mistaken revisions of Marxism, is actually neither Liu Shao-ch'i nor Lin Piao, but Mao Tse-tung!

In this respect, with a view to masking his ugly and vicious face in seizing power and waging rebellions and in making Liu Shao-ch'i and Lin Piao, whose "usefulness" was exhausted, totally responsible for all mistakes and failures, Mao Tse-tung resorted at first to utilizing criticism of the so-called Chinese Khrushchev in dealing with Liu Shao-ch'i and deliberately let the masses follow through with muddleheaded criticism. As soon as public opinion was created among the masses, direct criticism of Liu Shao-ch'i as the biggest powerholder walking the capitalist path within the party and attribution of the responsibility for all mistakes and failures before the Great Cultural Revolution to the person of Liu Shao-ch'i became possible. Nor did he [Mao] treat Lin Piao any differently. He initially used criticism referring to Lin Piao as being of "Liu Shao-ch'i's ilk" and then let the masses follow through with muddleheaded criticism. As soon as public opinion was created among the masses, he made public, direct criticism of the "mangled body and broken bones" of Lin Piao [referring to Lin's death in an airplane crash on September 13, 1971] and attributed all fascist criminal activities during the Great Cultural Revolution to the person of Lin Piao.

Nevertheless—the method is immaterial—after the overthrow of Liu Shao-ch'i, Mao Tse-tung termed Liu Shao-ch'i the biggest revisionist within the party and stated, after the episode of Lin Piao's "mangled body and broken bones" when the deceased could not give contrary evidence, that he [Mao] was "forced to scale the Liang Mountains" by Lin Piao and that Lin Piao "borrowed help from Chung K'uei [the demon killer, that is, Mao] in order to beat up devils."[2] But Mao Tse-tung was in direct command during the tenures of both Liu Shao-ch'i and Lin Piao as vice-chairman. Since Liu Shao-ch'i served as Mao Tse-tung's aide for a rather long time and Lin Piao as Mao Tse-tung's aide for quite a few years, Mao Tse-tung can never evade his responsibility for the party's erroneous revisions in the development of Marxism, as well as for every mistake committed by it in theory and in practice. Moreover, under Mao Tse-tung's villainous work style of replacing truth by might, both Liu Shao-ch'i and Lin Piao had no choice but to flatter and promote the line of the Thought of Mao Tse-tung. How on earth could they have had the courage to make their own decisions and act by themselves! Hence, after clarifying the problem, [we see that] Mao Tse-tung is undoubtedly the biggest revisionist within the party.

At this point, we may reach another conclusion; namely, during the past decade the deviation of "opposing only the corrupt official, but not the emperor" emerged, as illustrated in the first struggle against Liu Shao-ch'i and the second struggle against Lin Piao. Since this is a relatively confusing and complicated question, let us hope that every comrade in the whole party and the whole army will certainly conduct repeated discussions until this question is thoroughly clarified.

Now we shall speak of the severe revisionist mistakes committed by Mao Tse-tung in recent years with respect to the development of Marxism.

During the work conference of the Central Committee at Pei-tai-ho in August and the Tenth Plenum of the party's Eighth Central Committee in September 1962, Mao Tse-tung made two talks that have been glorified as being of great historical significance. In these two talks, Mao Tse-tung repeated his viewpoint of "On the Correct Handling of Contradictions Among the People" of February 27, 1957, while summing up the practical experience of socialism during the past half century and putting forth the basic line in the entire socialist historical stage. He stated:

Socialist society is a relatively long historical stage. In this historical stage of socialism, classes, class contradictions, and class struggles still exist; the struggles between the two roads of socialism and capitalism still exist; and the dangers of restoration of capitalism still exist. The durability and complexity of these struggles must be recognized.

On June 14, 1963, under the personal direction and cognizance of Mao Tse-tung, a document entitled "Suggestions on the General Line of the International Communist Movement" was published, which pointed out: "In the very long historical stage after the seizure of political power by the proletariat, the continuation of the class struggle still depends on objective laws that cannot be changed in accordance with human will."

During July 1964, before the launching of the rural Socialist Education movement, Mao Tse-tung said: "In the political and ideological domain, the outcome of the struggle between socialism and capitalism takes a very long time to come to a head. It cannot materialize in several decades and necessitates one to several hundred years before its completion."

In Mao Tse-tung's talks while touring various places from mid-August to September 12, 1971, he reiterated this in order to sum up the ten struggles over the party line during the past fifty years:

> We have sung the "Internationale" for fifty years, and our party has experienced ten schisms. I think that there will still be ten, twenty, and thirty occasions. Do you believe it? If you do not, I still believe it. Is there no struggle when communism is realized? I do not believe it. When communism is realized, struggles will still exist—struggles between new and old, between right and wrong. After many thousand years, it will still not be all right to commit mistakes and what is wrong will not be able to stand on its own feet (1972 party Central Committee document, Chung-fa no. 12).

Here Mao Tse-tung not only affirms the longevity of class struggle, but also asserts that classes, class contradictions, and class struggles still exist in communist society. He even stresses that the same circumstances will exist after many thousand years. In other words, communism will exist under a new kind of social system, which will still be unable to eliminate class exploitation, even after many thousand years. Consider that our country is already a relatively ancient state with a relatively long history, but up to now it is only over 5,000 years old. At present, China has been a socialist state for over twenty years. If it still will not be truly able to carry out communism, what historical significance can be attached to the proletarian revolution? Don't such mistaken conclusions of Mao Tse-tung completely deny the historical inevitability of Marxism, the possibility of the universal, worldwide realization of Marxism, the scientific basis of Marxism, and the scientific basis of the world proletarian revolutionary movement?

Here we must recognize that Liu Shao-ch'i's views on the extinction of the class struggle are a rightist reflection of the "hopelessness of the class struggle," a sentiment aimed at restoring a capitalist society; while Mao Tse-tung's mistaken conclusions on the continuation of the class struggle for many thousand years are a "leftist" reflection of the "hopelessness of the class struggle," aimed at restoring a feudal-slave society.

But they share one point. Both would lead the proletarian revolutionary movement in the contrary direction. Yet in terms of appearance and manner, Mao Tse-tung is more leftist in "form" and more rightist in "substance" than Liu Shao-ch'i and Lin Piao.

Because of Mao Tse-tung's continuing pretext that "the road is circuitous," the masses find it difficult to expose his various malicious and erroneous revisions of Marxism.

Not only are the masses easily puzzled by his superficial approach when he manifests an excessively leftist appearance and manner, but also when he manifests an extremely rightist appearance and manner, the masses do not easily guess the true nature of the nostrum he sells.

In 1847, Marx and Engels pointed out in the "Communist Manifesto" that "the union of education and material life are one of the indispensable instruments for changing the entire mode of production after the seizure of political power by the proletariat." Lenin once stated: "Enthusiasm cannot be relied on to build socialism; building socialism depends on the concern for and the individual interest of the proletariat." But Mao Tse-tung asserts that the existence of "poor staffs" [paupers] is a good thing. He completely disregards the need to support the laboring masses materially and misconstrues concern for the laboring masses and care for individual interest as "economism" and "revisionism." Through merely political studies in the educational domain that ignore the objective situation, he demands—really compels—the laboring masses to rely on "a wave of passion," "a bundle of energy," "no fear of hardship," and "no fear of death" in the cause of building socialism, an act that culminates in the total divorce of the party from the masses. The party and the laboring masses each walks a separate path, the masses continuously on strike and discontented, and the People's Liberation Army stationed indefinitely in factories everywhere. The resulting razor-edge struggle has directly alerted us to the severity of the current problem.

Marx and Engels's thesis of class struggle has been termed "scientific socialism" and differs from "idealistic socialism" since it requires a sound grasp of the laws of nature and social development that show that a capitalist society must become a socialist society due to the class struggle of the proletariat. If the laboring masses in a socialist society are to be as oppressed and exploited as in a capitalist society, no socialist society can ever be built.

Engels has pointed out: "If the state intervenes in the economy, no matter under whose ownership, only for the interest of the capitalists, exploitation will not be extinguished and only its form will be changed." Although the socialist reform of ownership of the means of production in our country is said to have been basically completed, the livelihood of the laboring people has not yet been consistently improved to a reasonable degree. On the contrary, the line of Mao Tse-tung makes use of banal egalitarianism or even reverse egalitarianism, bringing the standard of living of the more capable, meritorious, and affluent people down to that of the less capable, meritorious, and affluent people among the masses, thus deceptively depressing the standard of living of the laboring people. Not only was this true in the case of the [1962] Four Purities movement, but the same is also true of the current [1975] Restriction of Bourgeois Rights movement.[3] Naturally, many among the masses have condemned our [socialist] reform of ownership of the means of production as [only] a change from the ownership of the Kuomintang and the landlord–rich peasant class to that of the Communist party.[4] They have censured our reform, socialist ownership of the means of production, as a mere pretext for using collective ownership and total ownership for "turning public things into private" so that a few people will become a privileged class that rises above the people, and as contrary to the people's interest, as well as [for creating] a new aristocratic clique and a new exploiting class. Many people even clamor that the proletariat will launch another liberation struggle. Are these facts not sufficient to cause people to reflect deeply?

Although Mao Tse-tung's demands that the masses rely on "passion," "energy," "no fear of hardship" and "no fear of death," "build[ing] socialism," and the 1962 "Four Purities movement," as well as the current "Restriction of Bourgeois Rights movement," are excessively "leftist" on the surface, yet such revisions of Marxism are not intended to advance, develop, and accelerate the socialist construction of our country from the "leftist" direction, but to enhance the oppression and exploitation of the laboring masses so that social conditions in our country will retrogress to those of two thousand years ago and the Ch'in Shih-huang mode of feudal-slave society that levied heavy taxes and accumulated oppressive tributes will be restored.

Based on the theory and practice of Marxism, we can conclude that the "Thought of Mao Tse-tung" and the "line of Mao Tse-tung" that result from Mao Tse-tung's erroneous revisions of Marxism are completely alien to the framework of Marxism and are diametrically opposed to it. In dealing with this problem, we must effectively utilize the ideology and method of "one divided into two" in order to reveal Mao's ugly and vicious face. This important question affects the future of our country's proletarian revolution, and we hope that our comrades in the whole party and the whole army will hold serious discussions so that our understanding is clarified and a correct Marxist line achieved.

Since 1970, Mao Tse-tung has suddenly become surprisingly "rightist" in his diplomatic policy. Under the camouflage of the so-called revolutionary, diplomatic line of the Thought of Mao Tse-tung, invitations have continuously been extended to the bourgeois representatives of capitalist countries in the East and West and even to the chieftains of U.S. imperialism to visit our country. Perhaps we are all puzzled at this change in Mao Tse-tung; it is not worth a penny when the truth is revealed. Mao Tse-tung's recent invitation to U.S. imperialism's chieftain Ford to visit our country is meaningless to the socialist revolution and socialist construction of our country—apart from the fact that he [Mao] used this to show that he is capable of doing whatever he desires over the heads of 800 million Chinese laboring masses.

Nevertheless, as a result of such surprisingly "rightist" manifestations in the diplomatic line, we can arrive at one fact that demonstrates Mao Tse-tung's constant instability, total confusion, and lack of definite standards. Formerly, Liu Shao-ch'i's diplomatic line of "three reconciliations and one reduction" was termed bourgeois "peaceful transition" and "revisionist" and was repeatedly reviled.[5] But during recent years, Mao Tse-tung has befriended and collaborated with bourgeois countries in the East and West, as well as with U.S. imperialism, and has kept abreast of the "coexistence" diplomatic line of Soviet revisionist social-imperialism.[6] Is this not pursuing revisionism and peaceful coexistence? If Mao Tse-tung can pursue it now, why could Liu Shao-ch'i not pursue it formerly?

Since Mao's usurpation of the authority of the party's Central Committee, he has replaced truth by might and has, in theory and in practice, persistently worn the garb of Marxism to walk a path contrary to Marxism, with himself as the center—so that our socialist revolution has continuously marched backward and our party has become a party of family members, father and son, as well as a party of a handful of hereditary, new aristocratic cliques; the People's Liberation Army has become a fascist army that suppresses the revolutionary rebels of the working class and the peasantry; our society has become a feudal-slave society of the era of Ch'in Shih-huang; our country has become a country of feudalist society and fascist dictatorship; the proletarian dictatorship of our country has become a dictatorship of Mao Tse-tung over the people of the entire country.

> He is an [ungrateful] Chung-shan wolf;
> Success will turn him loose.[7]

No gift is more appropriate for Mao Tse-tung than these two lines of poetry. Lin Piao committed many mistakes after 1966, but before the "mangled body and broken bones" episode, he called Mao Tse-tung the "Ch'in Shih-huang of the contemporary era," which is indeed correct.

In general, for the present purpose of saving our party and our socialist revolutionary enterprise, we wish not only to criticize and overthrow Liu Shao-ch'i and Lin Piao, but also to concentrate all efforts on criticizing and overthrowing the biggest revisionist within the party—Mao Tse-tung! We hope that our comrades in the whole party and the whole army will unite and exert themselves toward this common objective.

With the most respectful salute of the revolution,

THE CENTRAL EXTRAORDINARY
COMMITTEE OF THE COMMUNIST
PARTY OF CHINA[8]

Quotations from Chairman Mao on Revolutionary Diplomacy

(The People's Press, Peking, June 1977)

DOCUMENT TWO

Workers of All Countries, Unite![1]

PUBLICATION NOTE

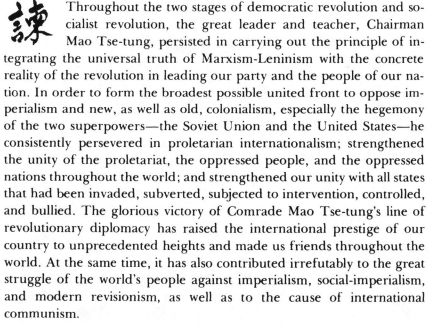Throughout the two stages of democratic revolution and socialist revolution, the great leader and teacher, Chairman Mao Tse-tung, persisted in carrying out the principle of integrating the universal truth of Marxism-Leninism with the concrete reality of the revolution in leading our party and the people of our nation. In order to form the broadest possible united front to oppose imperialism and new, as well as old, colonialism, especially the hegemony of the two superpowers—the Soviet Union and the United States—he consistently persevered in proletarian internationalism; strengthened the unity of the proletariat, the oppressed people, and the oppressed nations throughout the world; and strengthened our unity with all states that had been invaded, subverted, subjected to intervention, controlled, and bullied. The glorious victory of Comrade Mao Tse-tung's line of revolutionary diplomacy has raised the international prestige of our country to unprecedented heights and made us friends throughout the world. At the same time, it has also contributed irrefutably to the great struggle of the world's people against imperialism, social-imperialism, and modern revisionism, as well as to the cause of international communism.

The greatest theoretical contributions of Comrade Mao Tse-tung's line of revolutionary diplomacy are to sum up systematically the experience of the struggle of the proletariat in our country and in the world against imperialism and the reactionaries of various countries, to analyze the general situation of the proletarian revolution in the world during the current stage, and to set forth the scientific conclusion of the division of the globe into three worlds. His theory not only points out the basic road to consolidating the proletarian dictatorship, to forestalling the restoration of capitalism, and to building up socialism, but is also of great and profound world significance.

In looking back at the fighting records of the people of our country in opposing imperialism, revisionism, and reactionaries and in supporting the people's revolution in the world, we see that our resistance against the United States and our aid to Korea, as well as the protection of the homeland and defense of the country, were necessary to fulfill our obligation of internationalism. The mutual aid and support between us and the people of the three states of Vietnam, Cambodia, and Laos are also crucial to carrying out our requisite obligation of internationalism. The well-known five principles of peaceful coexistence initiated by us have served as the yardstick for relations between states and have exerted a profound impact on the international scene. We have adopted the eight principles of our country's foreign aid policy and have promoted the unity of the entire Third World against imperialism, and these principles are still praised by people today.[2]

The two superpowers, the Soviet Union and the United States, are currently the biggest international oppressors and exploiters, and the danger of a new world war emanates from these two hegemonies, especially from the social-imperialism of the Soviet Union. We have persistently opposed the aggressive and warlike policies of U.S. imperialism and social-imperialism; we have supported the anti-imperialism and antihegemony struggle of the revolutionary people of the entire world; and we have maintained the sovereignty and territorial integrity of our country.

For over twenty years, Comrade Mao Tse-tung's line of revolutionary diplomacy has consistently occupied a dominant position and produced achievements of lasting significance in the field of foreign relations of our country. After the publication of volume 5 of the *Selected Works of Mao Tse-tung*, we have edited Comrade Mao Tse-tung's utterances concerning the line of revolutionary diplomacy in order to publish them.

As far as the people of our country and various countries in the world are concerned, these publications should be read by everyone.

COMMITTEE FOR EDITING AND
PUBLISHING THE *Works of
Chairman Mao Tse-tung,*
CENTRAL COMMITTEE OF THE
COMMUNIST PARTY OF CHINA

June 1, 1977

1. THE CHINESE REVOLUTION IS PART OF THE WORLD REVOLUTION

The correct thesis that "the Chinese revolution is part of the world revolution" was put forward as early as 1924–1927 during the period of China's First Great Revolution. ("On New Democracy" [January 1940], in *Selected Works of Mao Tse-tung* [hereafter, *SWM*], 2: 662.)

There are two kinds of world revolution. The first belongs to the bourgeois or capitalist category. The era of this kind of world revolution is long past, having ended as far back as 1914 when the first imperialist world war began, and more particularly in 1917 when the October Revolution occurred. The second kind, namely, the proletarian-socialist world revolution, thereupon began. This revolution has the proletariat of the capitalist countries as its main force and the oppressed peoples of the colonies and semicolonies as its allies. (Ibid., in *SWM*, 2: 644.)

Marx says: "The proletariat must liberate not only itself, but also the whole of mankind. Unless it can liberate the whole of mankind, the proletariat cannot ultimately liberate itself. All comrades should note this principle." ("Letter to Red Guards of Tsinghua University Middle School" [August 1, 1966].)

Generally speaking, whether in China or any other country in the world, over 90 percent of the people will in the end support Marxism-Leninism. There are many people in the world who, having been hoodwinked by the social democratic parties, revisionism, imperialism, and the reactionaries in various countries, are not yet awake. But they will gradually wake up and support Marxism-Leninism. The truth of Marxism-Leninism is irresistible. The masses of the people wish to wage revolution, and world revolution will triumph. ("Speech at the Enlarged Central Work Conference" [January 30, 1962].)

Comrade Norman Bethune, a member of the Communist Party of Canada, was over fifty when he was sent by the communist parties of Canada and the United States to China; he made light of traveling thousands of miles to help us in our War of Resistance against Japan. He arrived in Yenan in the spring of last year [1938], went to work in the Wutai mountains, and to our great sorrow died a martyr at his post. What kind of spirit is this that makes a foreigner selflessly adopt the cause of the Chinese people's liberation as his own? It is the spirit of internationalism, the spirit of communism, from which every Chinese communist must learn. ("In Memory of Norman Bethune" [December 21, 1939], in *SWM*, 2: 653.)

We must unite with the proletariat of all capitalist countries, with the proletariat of Japan, Britain, the United States, Germany, Italy, and all other capitalist countries, for this is the only way to overthrow imperialism, to liberate our nation and people, and to liberate the other nations and peoples of the world. This is our internationalism, the internationalism with which we oppose both narrow nationalism and narrow patriotism. (Ibid., in *SWM*, 2: 653.)

We must always persevere in the principle of the unity of proletarian internationalism. We consistently advocate that socialist countries and the world communist movement must be solidly united on the basis of Marxism-Leninism. ("Speech at the Enlarged Central Work Conference" [January 30, 1962].)

In the past, Marxism-Leninism guided the world revolution from the standpoint of theory. Now something has been added to aid the world revolution from the standpoint of substance. This is the great achievement of Stalin. ("Speech at the Meeting of Various Walks of Life in Yenan in Celebration of Stalin's 60th Birthday" [December 21, 1939].)

The thoroughgoing liberation of oppressed people must first be based on their own struggles and then on international assistance. People who have achieved victory in revolution should help people who are seeking liberation. This is our internationalist obligation. ("Talk at the Reception for African Friends" [August 8, 1963].)

"Victory is possible even without international help." This is a mistaken idea. In the epoch of imperialism, a genuine people's revolution in any country cannot be victorious without help from the international revolutionary forces. Even if victory were won, it could not be consolidated. ("On the People's Democratic Dictatorship" [June 30, 1949], in *SWM*, 4: 1,478.)

It must not be assumed that the new system can be completely consolidated the moment it is established; that is impossible. It has to be consolidated step by step. To achieve its ultimate consolidation, it is necessary not only to bring about the socialist industrialization of the country and persevere in the socialist revolution on the economic front, but also to carry on constant and arduous socialist revolutionary struggles and socialist education on the political and ideological fronts. Moreover, various complementary international conditions are required. ("Speech at the Chinese Communist Party's National Conference on Propaganda Work" [March 12, 1957], in *SWM*, 5: 404.)

Unite in a common struggle with those nations of the world that treat us as equals and unite with the peoples of all countries; this means to ally ourselves with the Soviet Union, with the people's democracies, and with the proletariat and the broad masses of the people in all other countries to form an international united front. ("On the People's Democratic Dictatorship" [June 30, 1949], in *SWM*, 4: 1,477.)

The problem of the united front is whether to be anti-imperialist. All those who are anti-imperialist must be united. As far as the bourgeois democratic revolution is concerned, we must determine whether a person is anti-imperialist. The establishment of truly (not nominally) socialist countries and of the economy of the total people's ownership and collective ownership under proletarian leadership are different matters. These concern not only the interests of imperialism, but also those of the bourgeoisie. ("Talk at the Reception for the Zanzibar Expert M. M. Ali and His Wife" [June 18, 1964].)

Internationally, we must unite with all peace-loving and freedom-loving countries and peoples, beginning with the Soviet Union and the new democracies, so that we shall not stand alone in our struggle to safeguard these fruits of victory and to thwart the restorationist plots of domestic and foreign enemies. As long as we persist in the people's democratic dictatorship and unite with our foreign friends, we shall always be victorious. ("The Chinese People Have Stood Up!" [September 21, 1949], in *SWM*, 5: 5–6.)

Our China not only is the political center of the world revolution, but must also become the military and technological center of the world revolution. We can give arms to the world revolution. We can do so openly, even if the arms are inscribed with [Chinese] characters. Yes, we will openly support revolutionaries and become the arsenal of the world revolution. ("The Great Strategic Plan" [September 1967].)

2. LEARN FROM THE SOVIET UNION

The Chinese found Marxism through the Russians. Before the October Revolution, the Chinese were not only ignorant of Lenin and Stalin, they did not even know of Marx and Engels. The salvos of the October Revolution brought us Marxism-Leninism. The October Revolution helped progressives in China, as elsewhere throughout the world, to adopt the proletarian world outlook as the instrument for studying a nation's destiny and considering anew its own problems. Follow the path of the Russians—that was the progressives' conclusion. ("On the People's Democratic Dictatorship" [June 30, 1949], in *SWM*, 4: 1,475–76.)

Profound friendship exists between the people of the two great countries of China and the Soviet Union. After the October socialist revolution, the Soviet government was the first to abrogate, on the basis of the policy of Lenin and Stalin, the unequal treaties signed with China during the era of czarist Russia. For some thirty years, the people and government of the Soviet Union have aided the cause of liberation of the Chinese people on several occasions. The fraternal friendship received by the Chinese people in times of hardship from the people and government of the Soviet Union will never be forgotten. ("Speech on Arrival at the Station in Moscow" [December 16, 1949].)

I think we have been right in promoting the slogan of learning from other countries. The leaders of some countries are currently cautious about and even afraid of mentioning this slogan. It takes a little courage because theatrical pretensions must be discarded. ("On the Ten Major Relationships" [April 25, 1956], in *SWM*, 5: 285.)

We can consult the advanced experience of the Soviet Union. In past decades, all those who were anti-Soviet did not end well. ("Concerning the Anti-Chinese Problem" [March 22, 1960].)

We must be friendly with the Soviet Union, the people's democratic countries, and the communist parties and proletariat in various countries. To speak of internationalism and to learn from the good points of the Soviet Union and other foreign countries are matters of principle. ("Speech at the Chengtu Conference" [March 10, 1958].)

We must enable our comrades to understand that even one's ancestors had defects. We must analyze and not be so superstitious. As for the Soviet experience, all good things should be accepted and all bad things rejected. Now that we have learned a few skills, we can to some degree understand the Soviet Union as well as ourselves. (Ibid.)

We believe in Marxism, and we do not mechanically transplant Soviet experience. To transplant Soviet experience mechanically is erroneous. ("Directive at the Symposium for a Few Delegates to the First Session of the Committee of the Second National Industry and Commerce Association Conference" [December 8, 1956].)

Was the Hungarian incident beneficial? Since the problem was inevitable, it was good that it erupted. Pus must erupt from pustules. Those [communist] countries did not do their work well and always copied the Soviet Union without considering the concrete situation. The lesson of this incident is that we must act by integrating the universal truth of Marxism-Leninism with the concrete situation in China. (Ibid.)

In 1956, we not only cheered but also feared the criticism of Stalin. To take the lid off and get rid of superstitions and to release the pressure and liberate thought are entirely necessary. But we cannot agree with killing him off with one shot. ("Speech at the Chengtu Conference" [March 10, 1958].)

In the past, the Soviet Union was very friendly to us. After the Twentieth Congress in 1956, it began to be unfriendly. Later, with the worsening of relations, it withdrew over one thousand experts from China and abrogated several hundred contracts altogether. It began opposing the Communist Party of China openly. Since you [the Russians] voice opposition, we must open the debate. Presently they [the Russians] are again asking us to stop the open debate, perhaps for three months. We state that even three days are impossible. ("Talk at the Reception for Sasaki Kōzō, Kuroda Hisao, and Hososako Kanemitsu of the Japan Socialist Party" [July 10, 1964].)

As for the problem of international relations, we cannot follow blindly in those areas where we have gained experience. The Soviet Union has initiated extensive criticism, which in some matters is not applicable to our country or to the Soviet Union. We are mindful of the many mistakes committed by their vertical leadership. For instance, in the matter of purges, we do not arrest the majority or kill a single person. It is debatable whether the unified command is based on the military viewpoint, whether the mass line is a matter of grace, or whether capital is to be accumulated by means of price disparities between industrial goods and agricultural products or by taxation. But we do not state that there is nothing to learn from the Soviet Union; there are many things worth studying. It is the Soviet Union that helps us construct our state, and after all any socialist country is good. There is presently only one such country. Though faulty, it is still very worthy of our study. We must not follow blindly and should analyze everything. Since it may be fragrant or foul to break wind, we cannot say that the Soviet Union breaks only fragrant wind. Now that others call it foul, we also follow suit. All that is useful must be learned; the good things of capitalism should also be studied. ("Speech at the Enlarged Meeting of the Central Politburo" [April 1956].)

No matter when, whether now or in the future, we of this generation and our offspring must learn from the Soviet Union and study the Soviet experience. Not to learn from the Soviet Union is to commit a mistake. People will ask: since the Soviet Union is ruled by revisionism, are we still to learn [from it]? What we study are the good people and good things of the Soviet Union, as well as the good experiences of the Soviet party. As for the bad people and bad things of the Soviet Union, as well as the revisionists of the Soviet Union, we should treat them as teachers by negative example from whom we shall draw our lessons. ("Speech at the Enlarged Central Work Conference" [January 30, 1962].)

All foreign countries, no matter how small, must be treated with equality; do not crow. Even though we are not imperialists and had no October Revolution, we cannot crow from the start. But we may crow as soon as we have learned something. ("Speech at the Enlarged Meeting of the Central Politburo" [April 1956].)

3. THE TWO CAMPS

The truth of Marxism is manifold; it may be summed up in one basic sentence: "To rebel is right." For several thousand years, it was always stated: "To oppress is right; to exploit is right; to rebel is not right." Since Marxism emerged, this old judgment has been reversed. This is a great achievement. This truth was derived from the proletariat's struggle and was summed up by Marx. Out of this truth arise resistance, struggle, and socialism. What was Comrade Stalin's achievement? It was to expound this truth and Marxism-Leninism and, for the sake of the oppressed people in the whole world, to set forth a lucid, concrete, and vivid truth: namely, to establish a comprehensive theory for establishing a revolutionary front and overthrowing imperialism and capitalism, as well as for building a socialist society. ("Speech at the Meeting of Various Walks of Life in Yenan in Celebration of Stalin's 60th Birthday" [December 21, 1939].)

At present, the world is divided into two fronts of struggle: one is imperialism, which is the front oppressing the people; the other is socialism, which is the front resisting oppression. ("Talk at the Reception of Returned Students and Trainees of Our Country in Moscow" [November 17, 1957].)

The two fronts of revolution and counterrevolution must each have a chief or commandant. Who is the commandant of the front of counterrevolution? It is imperialism or Chamberlain. Who is the commandant of the front of revolution? It is socialism or Stalin. Comrade Stalin is the leader of the world revolution. This is a very important matter. Out of all mankind this man Stalin emerges; this is a big event. With him around, things become manageable. As you know, Marx is dead, Engels is dead, and Lenin is also dead. If there were no Stalin, who could issue orders? It is really fortunate that there is a Soviet Union, a communist party, and also a Stalin in the world at present so that affairs of this world become manageable. What does the commandant of the revolution do? He enables everyone to have food to eat, clothes to wear, housing to inhabit, and books to study. In order to do so, he has to lead over one billion people in waging the struggle against the oppressors until the final victory. This is what Stalin has to carry out. ("Speech at the Meeting of Various Walks of Life in Yenan in Celebration of Stalin's 60th Birthday [December 21, 1939].)

The whole world will be swept into one or the other of these two fronts, and "neutrality" will then be merely a deceptive term. This is especially true of China, which, fighting an imperialist power that has penetrated deep into its territory, cannot conceive of ultimate victory without the assistance of the Soviet Union. ("On New Democracy" [January 1940], in *SWM*, 2: 683.)

After the nationwide victory of the Chinese revolution and the solution of the land problem, two basic contradictions will still exist in China. The first is internal, namely, the contradiction between the working class and the bourgeoisie. The second is external, namely, the contradiction between China and the imperialist countries. ("Report to the Second Plenum of the Seventh Central Committee of the Communist Party of China" [March 5, 1949], in *SWM*, 4: 1,434.)

In your view, will socialism be successfully realized? Do you have buckets? Have you drawn water [from the well] by fifteen buckets, [feeling uneasy] with seven up and eight down? Do you fear that socialism will not be successfully realized and that the socialist camp will collapse? In my view, even if it collapses, it will be unimportant and inconsequential. In my view, it will not collapse. The socialist camp consists primarily of the Soviet Union and China. The policy of drawing China and the Soviet Union together is correct. Even now some people doubt this policy, stating: "Do not lean toward each other." They still consider it possible to adopt a midway position between the Soviet Union and the United States and to serve as a bridge, that is, to emulate the ways of Yugoslavia. Is this [taking money from both sides] a good way? I regard this midway position as neither good nor beneficial to the nation because on the one side stands a powerful imperialist, and we Chinese have long been oppressed by imperialists. If we stand between the Soviet Union and the United States, it looks very good and independent but is not so in reality. Since the United States is unreliable, it will give you something but not very much. How could the United States completely feed [all of] us? Imperialists cannot feed you to the full, and they always oppress Asia, Africa, and Latin America. India has been oppressed for over two hundred years, and they [the Indians] have never had a hearty meal. Imperialists are pennypinchers. Imperialists—Britain, the United States, France, Holland, and other countries—sent the joint eight-nation expedition that burned our Yüan-ming-yüan [Imperial Summer Palace in Peking] and seized our Hong Kong and Taiwan. Since Hong Kong belongs to us Chinese, why was it ceded? Why was the Bandung Conference [1954] able to unite the countries of Asia and Africa? It was because imperialism deliberately oppressed others. This imperialist is the United States. ("Directive at the Symposium for a Few Delegates to the First Session of the Committee of the Second National Industry and Commerce Association Conference" [December 8, 1956].)

As things are today, it is perfectly clear that unless there is a policy of alliance with Russia, with the land of socialism, there will inevitably be a policy of alliance with imperialism, with the imperialist powers. ("On New Democracy" [January 1940], in *SWM*, 2: 683.)

"You are leaning to one side." Exactly. Sun Yat-sen's 40 years of experience [1885–1925] and the Communist party's 28 years of experience [1921–1949] have taught us to lean to one side. In the light of the experiences accumulated in these 40 years and these 28 years, all Chinese without exception must lean either to the side of imperialism or to the side of socialism. Sitting on the fence will not do, nor is there a third road. ("On the People's Democratic Dictatorship" [June 30, 1949], in *SWM*, 4: 1,477–78.)

Who designed and equipped so many important factories for us? Was it the United States? Or Britain? No, neither the one nor the other. Only the Soviet Union was willing to do so because it is a socialist country and our ally. In addition to the Soviet Union, the fraternal countries in East Europe have also given us some assistance. ("On the Correct Handling of Contradictions Among the People" [February 27, 1957], in *SWM*, 5: 401.)

Internationally, we belong to the side of the anti-imperialist front headed by the Soviet Union, and so we can turn only to this side for genuine and friendly help, not to the side of the imperialist front. ("On the People's Democratic Dictatorship" [June 30, 1949], in *SWM*, 4: 1,480.)

We consider that strengthening the unification of various socialist countries headed by the Soviet Union is the sacred national obligation of all socialist countries. ("Speech at the U.S.S.R. Supreme Soviet Meeting in Celebration of the 40th Anniversary of the October Socialist Revolution" [November 6, 1957].)

To strengthen our solidarity with the Soviet Union, to strengthen our solidarity with all socialist countries—that is our fundamental policy, this is where our basic interests lie. ("On the Correct Handling of Contradictions Among the People" [February 27, 1957], in *SWM*, 5: 402.)

In the international sphere we must firmly unite with the Soviet Union, the people's democracies, and the forces of peace and democracy everywhere; there should not be the slightest hesitation or wavering on this question. ("Be a True Revolutionary" [June 23, 1950], in *SWM*, 5: 28.)

The First World War was followed by the birth of the Soviet Union, with a population of 200 million. The Second World War was followed by the emergence of the socialist camp, with a combined population of 900 million. If the imperialists insist on launching a third world war, it is certain that several hundred million more will turn to socialism, and then there will not be much room left on earth for the imperialists; it is also likely that the whole structure of imperialism will completely collapse. ("On the Correct Handling of Contradictions Among the People" [February 27, 1957], in *SWM*, 5: 398.)

The victory of the great October socialist revolution has made it certain that the people of the world will win victory, and today this prospect becomes nearer and more certain with the birth of the People's Republic of China and the people's democracies. ("Great Victories in Three Mass Movements" [October 23, 1951], in *SWM*, 5: 51.)

The direction of the wind in the world has changed. The struggle between the socialist camp and the capitalist camp is such that either the west wind prevails over the east wind or the east wind prevails over the west wind. At present, there are 2.7 billion people in the entire world, with nearly one billion people in the various socialist countries; more than 700 million people in the independent, former colonial countries; 600 million people in the countries now striving for independence or full independence, together with those capitalist countries not belonging to the imperialist camp; and no more than 400 million people in the imperialist camp, which is, moreover, divided. "Earthquakes" will occur. Now it is not the west wind that prevails over the east wind, but the east wind that prevails over the west wind. ("Talk at the Reception of Returned Students and Trainees of Our Country in Moscow" [November 17, 1957].)

As for relations between the imperialist countries and ourselves, they are among us and we are among them. We support the people's revolution in their countries, and they conduct subversive activities in ours. We have our men in their midst, that is, the Communists, the revolutionary workers, farmers, and intellectuals, and the progressives in their countries. They have their men in our midst; in China, for instance, there are among us many people from the bourgeoisie, the democratic parties, and the landlord class. ("Talks at a Conference of Secretaries of Provincial, Municipal, and Autonomous Region Party Committees" [January 1957], in *SWM* 5: 342.)

We are united with all Marxist-Leninists, all revolutionary comrades, and the entire people, and never with the anticommunists and antipeople imperialists or the reactionaries in various countries. If possible, we shall establish diplomatic relations with these people and seek peaceful coexistence on the basis of the five principles. But these affairs and our unity with the people of various countries are two completely different things. ("Speech at the Enlarged Central Work Conference" [January 30, 1962].)

4. THE TWO ROADS

The ideological and social system of capitalism has already become a museum piece in one part of the world (in the Soviet Union), while in other countries it resembles "a dying person who is sinking fast, like the sun setting beyond the western hills" and will soon be relegated to the museum. Only the communist ideological and social system is full of youth and vitality, sweeping the world with the momentum of an avalanche and the force of a thunderbolt. ("On New Democracy" [November 1940], in *SWM*, 2: 679.)

If we wish to overthrow a government, it is first necessary to create public opinion, to handle ideological conditions, and to take care of the superstructure. It is the same with revolution as with counterrevolution. Our ideological conditions enable us to carry out the revolutionary tenets of Marx and Lenin and to integrate the universal truth of Marxism-Leninism with the concrete reality of the Chinese revolution. If this integration goes well, the problem will be solved better. If not, failure and setback will ensue. ("Speech at the Tenth Plenum of the Eighth Central Committee" [September 24, 1962].)

We must firmly reject and criticize all decadent bourgeois systems, ideologies, and ways of life in foreign countries. But in no way should this prevent us from learning the advanced science and technology and the scientific aspects of enterprise management of capitalist countries. ("On the Ten Major Relationships" [April 25, 1956], in *SWM*, 5: 287.)

In our people's political activities, how should they judge whether a person's words and deeds are right or wrong? On the basis of the principles of our constitution, the will of the overwhelming majority of our people, and the common political positions that have been proclaimed on various occasions by our political parties, we consider that, broadly speaking, the criteria should be as follows:

1. Words and deeds should help to unite and not divide the people of all our nationalities.
2. They should be beneficial and not harmful to socialist transformation and socialist construction.
3. They should help to consolidate and not undermine or weaken the people's democratic dictatorship.
4. They should help to consolidate and not undermine or weaken democratic centralism.
5. They should help to consolidate and not shake off or weaken the leadership of the Communist Party.
6. They should be beneficial and not harmful to international socialist unity and the unity of the peace-loving people of the world.

Of these six criteria, the most important are the two about the socialist path and the leadership of the party. ("On the Correct Handling of Contradictions Among the People" [February 27, 1957], in *SWM*, 5: 393.)

The imperialists and the domestic reactionaries will certainly not take their defeat lying down; they will fight to the last ditch. After there is peace and order throughout the country, they are sure to engage in sabotage and to create disturbances by one means or another; every day and every hour they will attempt a comeback. This is inevitable and beyond all doubt; under no circumstances must we relax our vigilance. ("The Chinese People Have Stood Up!" [September 21, 1949], in *SWM*, 5: 5.)

Whoever sides with the revolutionary people is a revolutionary. Whoever sides with imperialism, feudalism, and bureaucratic capitalism is a counterrevolutionary. ("Be a True Revolutionary" [June 23, 1950], in *SWM*, 5: 26–27.)

After cooperation in agriculture is initiated, the worker-peasant alliance will eventually be consolidated on the basis of socialism. This new worker-peasant alliance will ultimately isolate the bourgeoisie. Capitalism will die out among the 600 million Chinese population. Some people state that we are without conscience; we say that Marxists have not much conscience toward the bourgeoisie, and the less conscience in this respect the better. A few of our comrades are too charitable. We wish to extinguish the bourgeoisie on the earth and transform them into a relic of history. This is very important and a very good thing. ("Summation at the Enlarged Meeting of the Sixth Plenum of the Seventh Central Committee of the Communist Party of China" [September 1955].)

Some among the democratic parties, nonparty democratic personages, the higher intellectuals, and religious, industrial, and commercial circles, along with a portion of the proletariat have illusions that the United States and Britain will help us. Let us propagandize about this well. Is it correct to lean to one side? We lean to one side in order to join with the Soviet Union on a basis of equality. We have not experienced those problems that occurred in Poland and Hungary. We believe in Marxism and do not mechanically transplant the Soviet experiences; to do so is erroneous. ("Directive at the Symposium for a Few Delegates to the First Session of the Committee of the Second National Industry and Commerce Association Conference" [December 8, 1956].)

Loans from a socialist country are different from those from an imperialist country. This statement accords with the facts, and socialist countries are, after all, better than capitalist countries. We understand this principle. The basic question is one of system, and the system determines the direction in which a country proceeds. The socialist system determines that socialist countries are always adverse to imperialist countries; compromises are always temporary. ("Notes on Reading the Soviet Work, *Political Economy* [1961–1962].)

We must unite with the Soviet Union, the fraternal parties, and the parties from 87 countries, no matter what names they have called us. Do not fear name-calling. Since the beginning of history, the Communist party has been called names. Not to be called names is not to be a Communist party. ("Speech at the Ninth Plenum of the Eighth Central Committee" [January 18, 1961].)

We should support whatever the enemy opposes and oppose whatever the enemy supports. ("Interview with Three Correspondents from the Central News Agency, the *Sao tang pao*, and the *Hsin min pao*" [September 16, 1939], in *SWM*, 2: 580.)

Some communist parties are opposed to our measures and say that we are no good. This is like imperialism, which also objects to our scheme of people's communes. Imperialism opposes us; so do the French Communists. There may be some advantages, although these are difficult to ascertain; for if there is no advantage, why should they oppose us? So we must welcome them [the French Communists]. This is to say, we shall walk not on the capitalist road but on the socialist road. ("Talk at the Reception for the Algerian Cultural Delegation" [April 15, 1964].)

What is revolution? Revolution is the proletariat's overthrow of the capitalist and the peasant's overturn of the landlord, followed by the establishment and consolidation of a worker-peasant coalition regime. At present, the revolutionary task has not yet been completed, and it is not certain who will overthrow whom. Isn't the Soviet Union still ruled by Khrushchev and the bourgeoisie? Some bourgeois also control political power in our country; some production teams, factories, county committees, district committees, and provincial committees as well have members belonging to the bourgeoisie; some deputy chiefs of the public security bureaus are also such people. Who leads culture? The movies and drama are both at the service of the bourgeoisie; they are not at the service of the majority of the people. ("Talk with Mao-Yüan-hsin" [Mao's nephew; March 1964].)

The Soviet Union wishes to pursue the road of capitalist restoration.

The United States very much welcomes this goal; so does Europe. We do not welcome it. ("Talk with French [Culture] Minister Malraux" [August 3, 1965].)

In Sino-Soviet relations, bickering always happens. Do not imagine that there can be no bickering in the world. Marxism is bickering-ism, for there are always contradictions. Contradictions produce struggles. Presently there is some bickering between China and the Soviet Union, but not much. We are even closer and more united than before. Their methods are not the same as ours. We must wait and do more work. ("Summation at the Conference of Secretaries of Provincial and Municipal Committees" [January 1957].)

5. THE TWO LINES

A word can make a state prosperous; a word can end a state. This is to change spirit into substance. In a few words, Marx wants the proletarian revolution and the dictatorship of the proletariat. Are these not words to turn a state toward prosperity? Khrushchev has also a few words, namely, do not wage class struggle or revolution. Are these not words to end a state? ("Speech at the Hangchow Conference" [May 1963].)

Both dogmatism and revisionism run counter to Marxism. Marxism must necessarily advance; it must develop along with practice and cannot stand still. It would become lifeless if it were stagnant and stereotyped. The basic principles of Marxism must, however, never be violated; otherwise mistakes will be made. Dogmatism is approaching Marxism from a metaphysical point of view and regarding it as something rigid. Revisionism is negating the basic principles of Marxism and negating its universal truth. Revisionism is one form of bourgeois ideology. The revisionists deny the differences between socialism and capitalism, between the dictatorship of the proletariat and the dictatorship of the bourgeoisie. What they advocate is, in fact, not the socialist line but the capitalist line. Under present circumstances, revisionism is more pernicious than dogmatism. One of the important tasks now confronting us on the ideological front is to criticize revisionism. ("Speech at the Chinese Communist Party's National Conference on Propaganda Work" [March 12, 1957], in *SWM*, 5: 417–18.)

Revisionism, or rightist opportunism, is a bourgeois trend of thought that is even more dangerous than dogmatism. The revisionists, the rightist opportunists, pay lip service to Marxism; they, too, attack "dogmatism." But what they are really attacking is the quintessence of Marxism. They oppose or distort materialism and dialectics, oppose or try to weaken the people's democratic dictatorship and the leading role of the Communist party, and oppose or try to weaken socialist transformation and socialist construction. ("On the Correct Handling of Contradictions Among the People" [February 27, 1957], in *SWM*, 5: 392.)

At present, a great many communist parties in the world are controlled by revisionist leaders. There are in the world over one hundred communist parties, which are now divided into two kinds of communist parties: the revisionist communist parties and the Marxist communist parties. ("Talk at the Reception for Sasaki Kōzō, Kuroda Hisao, and Hososako Kanemitsu of the Japan Socialist Party" [July 10, 1964].)

Another [country], namely Brazil, disapproves of us because we disagree with [the idea of] a peaceful transition. Several months ago, a coup d'etat that drove out the [Brazilian] president occurred. The leader of the revisionist party was sentenced to eight years in prison. This party leader, [Luiz Carlos] Prestes, who had visited China, was a very famous communist and later became a revisionist. American imperialism and its running dogs are not concerned whether you are a revisionist; they do not care. Among the nine Chinese arrested, six were [foreign] trade workers, and three were news reporters.

This is to say, revisionists do not oppose imperialism; they compromise with imperialism and reactionaries. ("Talk at the Reception for the Zanzibar Expert M. M. Ali and His Wife" [June 18, 1964].)

The Communist Party of Iraq in Asia is also anti-Chinese. They paid attention only to opposing the Communist Party of China and not to the crisis of a coup d'etat confronting themselves. During this past year, a coup d'etat occurred in which Qasim, as well as the general secretary of the party, was killed. (Ibid.)

Imperialism says that there is no question [of change] for us of the first generation, no [question of] change for the second generation, and some hope for the third and fourth generations. Can this hope of imperialism be realized? Is this statement of imperialism true? We hope that it will not become true, but it is possible. During the third generation in the Soviet Union, the revisionism of Khrushchev emerged, and we also may have revisionism. ("Speech on the Consolidation of Military Work and the Cultivation of Revolutionary Successors" [June 16, 1964].)

Stalin made a number of errors in connection with China. The "leftist" adventurism pursued by Wang Ming in the latter part of the Second Revolutionary Civil War period [1927–1937] and his rightist opportunism in the early days of the War of Resistance against Japan [1937–1945] can both be traced to Stalin. At the time of the War of Liberation, Stalin at first enjoined us not to pursue the revolution, maintaining that if civil war flared up, the Chinese nation would risk destroying itself. Then when fighting did erupt, he regarded us half seriously, half skeptically. When we won the war, Stalin suspected that ours was a Tito-type victory, and in 1949 and 1950 the pressure on us was indeed intense. ("On the Ten Major Relationships" [April 25, 1956], in *SWM*, 5: 286.)

The past few years were not very good, but the situation has begun improving. In 1959 and 1960, we committed a few mistakes, mainly due to the lack of comprehension and the inexperience of many people. The principal problem resulted from high levies and purchases. When there was not much grain, we insisted that there was, and recklessness took over. Recklessness took command of both agriculture and industry. Several grandiose operations were also mistakenly launched. The latter half of 1960 witnessed some corrections, which had begun as early as the First Chengchow Conference in October 1958. Later, the Wuchang Conference in November and December, the Third Chengchow Conference in February and March 1959, and the subsequent Shanghai Conference in April all paid attention to making corrections. During the interval, we did not sufficiently discuss this problem in the early part of 1960. Because revisionism had come to oppress us, we gave heed to opposing Khrushchev. Since the latter half of 1958, he had sought to blockade China's seacoast and to establish a joint fleet with our country for the sake of controlling the coast and blockading us. Khrushchev came to China because of this problem. Later, on the question of Sino-Indian borders in September 1959, Khrushchev supported Nehru in attacking us, and the Tass agency issued a statement to that effect. Subsequently, during the celebration banquet on the tenth anniversary of the founding of our nation, Khrushchev assailed us from our rostrum. Later, we were beseiged at the Bucharest Conference in 1960. Then at the conference of the two parties, the draft committee meeting of 26 countries, the Moscow conference of 81 countries, and the Warsaw conference, disputes between Marxism and revisionism occurred. In 1960, a battle was waged with Khrushchev. You see that these problems have occurred among socialist countries and within Marxism-Leninism; actually the roots are very deep, and the conflicts began long ago. China was not allowed to wage revolution. In 1945 Stalin tried to stop the Chinese revolution, saying that civil war could not be waged and cooperation must be carried out with Chiang Kai-shek lest the Chinese nation be extinguished. At that time, we did not implement his policy, and the revolution triumphed. After the victory of the revolution, he also suspected that China was like Yugoslavia and I would become a Tito. After my arrival in Moscow to conclude the Sino-Soviet treaty of alliance and mutual assistance, there was still a struggle. Stalin was unwilling to sign, but after two months of negotiations he finally signed. When did Stalin start to believe in us? It was after [the war of] resisting U.S. aggression and aiding Korea in the winter of 1950 that he believed that we were neither Tito nor Yugoslavia. But now we have still turned out to be "leftist adventurists . . . nationalists" and "dogmatists . . . sectarianists," but Yugoslavia has become "Marxist." At present, Yugoslavia is doing very well, is getting ahead, and is said to be "socialist." Thus, the socialist camp is complicated internally. But it is really simple, and there is only one truth: that is, the problem of class struggle, the problem of struggle between the proletariat and the bourgeoisie, the problem of struggle between Marxism and anti-Marxism, and the problem of struggle between Marxism and revisionism. ("Speech at the Tenth Plenum of the Eighth Central Committee" [September 24, 1962].)

Among the people of various countries, the masses of the people, who constitute more than 90 percent of the total population, always want revolution and support Marxism-Leninism. They will not support revisionism. Although some people temporarily support it, they will eventually give it up. They will gradually awaken, oppose imperialism and the reactionaries of various countries, and fight revisionism. A true Marxist-Leninist must stand firmly on the side of the masses of the people, who constitute more than 90 percent of the world population. ("Speech at the Enlarged Central Work Conference" [January 30, 1962].)

Khrushchev, in his revisionism, cursed us as sectarianists and sham revolutionaries. Good cursing. Not long ago, the Soviet Central Committee proposed four points in a letter to the Chinese Communist Central Committee: (1) stopping public polemics; (2) reassignment of experts; (3) Sino-Soviet border negotiations; and (4) expansion of trade. It is all right to conduct border negotiations, and they will start on February 25 [1964]. A little, but not too much, trade can take place. Soviet goods are heavy, bulky, and costly. We have to keep something up our sleeves. ("Summary of a Talk at the Spring Festival" [February 13, 1964].)

It is not easy to be a running dog; witness Nehru who is not prospering. Imperialism and revisionism have failed. Revisionism has run into a wall everywhere. In Romania, it does so. In Poland, it is ignored. In Cuba, it is half-obeyed and half-ignored. [Cuba] has no choice but to obey halfway, otherwise no oil or arms would be available. (Ibid.)

You see that we have waged a struggle with Khrushchev. Can victory be achieved? We have fought against enemies all our lives. Since we have dared to struggle against imperialism and have defeated imperialism, can we not defeat Khrushchev? We are struggling mainly against imperialism and revisionism. Reactionaries like Nehru are of no consequence! ("Aside During a Summing Up" [March 1964].)

Neither can we get along with the French Communist Party. They have not sent [us] a delegation either. The Communists are now disunited; their [internal] contradictions are slight, neither serious nor minor. This is natural. . . . They oppose us everyday, calling us dogmatists and Trotskyites. ("Talk at the Reception for the Algerian Cultural Delegation" [April 15, 1964].)

At present, the Soviet Union is a bourgeois dictatorship, a big bourgeois dictatorship, a German fascist dictatorship, a Hitler-like dictatorship, a bunch of rascals who are worse than de Gaulle. ("Aside During a Summing Up of the Leadership Group of the [State] Planning Commission" [May 11, 1964].)

The Soviet Union was the first socialist country, and the Communist Party of the Soviet Union was founded by Lenin. Although the party and state leadership of the Soviet Union is now usurped by revisionists, I wish to persuade you comrades to believe firmly that the majority of the Soviet Union's masses and party members, as well as cadres, are good and want to wage revolution. This revisionist rule will not last long. ("Speech at the Enlarged Central Work Conference" [January 30, 1962]).

The development of the new weapons, the guided missiles and the atom bombs, has progressed rapidly. The hydrogen bomb was completed in two years and eight months. Our development speed surpassed those of the United States, Britain, and France, and we rank fourth in the world in the great achievements of guided missiles and atom bombs. This is a consequence of Khrushchev's "assistance," which forced us to pursue our own path after he withdrew the [Soviet] experts. We must give him a medal weighing one ton. ("The Great Strategic Plan" [September 1967].)

6. NATIONALISM

Colonialism, nationalism, and communism constituted Leninism's formulas. ("Talk with the Directors of Various Cooperative Districts" [November 30, 1958].)

Any class, party, or individual in an oppressed nation that joins the revolution—whether it is conscious of the point or understands it—is, as long as it opposes imperialism, an ally of the proletarian-socialist world revolution, and its revolution is part of the proletarian-socialist world revolution. ("On New Democracy" [January 1940], in *SWM*, 2: 664.)

The national revolutionary front in colonies and semicolonies seems, according to some people, to stand in the middle [of the political spectrum]. Since its adversary is imperialism, it must claim socialism as a friend and belong to the side of the revolutionary front against the oppressor. ("Speech at the Meeting of Various Walks of Life in Yenan in Celebration of Stalin's 60th Birthday" [December 21, 1939].)

Is it true that there are no revolutionary fronts in the world other than this [proletarian-socialist] revolutionary front? Have 31 years of history [1917–1948] not proven that all those who are dissatisfied with imperialism or the Soviet Union and all those who belong to the so-called "middle line" and "third road" and attempt to stand midway between the imperialist counterrevolutionary front and the revolutionary front against imperialism and its running dogs in various nations are thoroughly deceitful and utterly bankrupt? ("Revolutionary Forces of the Whole World Unite, Fight Against Imperialist Aggression" [November 1948]. [This quotation is not included in the article of the same title in *SWM*, 4: 1359–62.])

All nationalities must trust one another. Regardless of nationality, all that matters is the truth. Marx was a Jew, and Stalin was from a minority group. ("Directive on the Problem of Nationalities" [March 1958].)

We Communists ignore questions of native place and nationality and ask only whether there is communism and how much communism there is. (Ibid.)

Ultimately, national struggle is a problem of class struggle. The oppressors of the black people in the United States consist only of the reactionary ruling bloc among the white race. They can never represent the overwhelming majority of workers, peasants, revolutionary intellectuals, and other enlightened persons among the white race. ("Statement in Support of the Just Struggle of the Black People in the United States Against Racial Discrimination" [August 8, 1963].)

I see that there are industries in Africa. There are many countries that have industries, including mines, railways, highways, and other industries, some of which were founded by imperialists and others by Africans themselves. At present, although no communist parties exist, there will eventually be a few. Yet it is not really true that no communist party exists. For example, there are communist parties in Algeria, Morocco, and South Africa. Yet the Algerian party is not a revolutionary but a revisionist party. A revisionist party such as the Algerian party is worse than the [Algerian] national liberation front, for the latter pursues wars of national liberation and the former, the Algerian Communist Party, opposes wars of liberation and obeys the orders of the French Communists. The Algerian Communist Party is opposed to us and is anti-Chinese. The Algerian government and national liberation front cooperate with us. ("Talk at the Reception for the Zanzibar Expert M. M. Ali and His Wife" [June 18, 1964].)

As long as imperialism, nationalism, and revisionism exist, whether they are capitalist countries, it will not be possible to solve the class problem. For this reason, it is our duty to resist imperialism and support national liberation movements, that is, to support the broad masses of the people in Asia, Africa, and Latin America, including workers, peasants, the revolutionary national bourgeoisie, and the revolutionary intelligentsia. We must be united with all these vast numbers of people. But these groups cannot include the reactionary national bourgeoisie like Nehru or reactionary bourgeois intellectuals, such as the Japanese communist renegade Kanga Shōjirō who advocates the theory of organizational reform, along with six or seven [other] persons. ("Speech at the Tenth Plenum of the Eighth Central Committee" [September 24, 1962].)

Are there classes in the socialist countries? We can now ascertain that as long as classes exist in the socialist countries, class struggle certainly exists. Lenin has said that after the victory of the revolution, the overthrown classes continue to give rise to the bourgeoisie because the bourgeoisie exists abroad and the remnants of the bourgeoisie, as well as of the petite bourgeoisie, at home. Thus, the overthrown bourgeoisie will still exist for a long time and may even be restored. The bourgeois revolutions in Europe, such as in England and France, were reversed several times. After feudalism's overthrow, it experienced several restorations and reversals. The socialist countries may witness this kind of reversal; for example, Yugoslavia has changed its nature and become revisionist—from a worker-peasant state to a state ruled by reactionary nationalistic elements. (Ibid.)

International revisionists continually curse us. Our attitude is to let them curse us, and we shall respond appropriately as necessary. Our party has become accustomed to being cursed. Without mentioning previous accusations, how do we fare now? The in perialists, reactionary nationalists, and revisionists revile us abroad: Chiang Kai-shek, the landlords, rich peasants, reactionaries, bad elements, and rightists curse us at home. They have cursed us like this since the beginning. ("Speech at the Enlarged Central Work Conference" [January 30, 1960].)

Oppressed people and nations can never distrust their own liberation to the "enlightenment" of imperialism and its running dogs; only through strengthened solidarity and persistent struggles can victory be achieved. ("Statement on Opposing United States/Diem Ngo Dinh Clique's Aggression and Massacre of the People in South Vietnam" [August 29, 1963].)

American imperialism massacres foreigners as well as white and black people at home, and Nixon's fascist brutality has lit the glowing fire of a revolutionary mass movement in the United States ("People of the Whole World Unite, Defeat the U.S. Aggressors and All Their Running Dogs" [May 20, 1970].)

7. IMPERIALISM

China must be independent. China must be liberated. China's affairs must be decided and managed by the Chinese people themselves; no further interference, not even the slightest, from any imperialist country will be tolerated. ("Address to the Preparatory Committee of the New Political Consultative Conference" [June 15, 1949], in *SWM*, 4: 1,469.)

The state is disposed to be a mechanism for suppressing antagonistic forces. Even if there is no need to suppress hostile forces at home, the state's disposition to suppress antagonistic forces abroad does not change. The so-called forms of the state comprise only the armed forces, prison, arrest, and execution of persons. As long as imperialism exists, will the form of the state be any different in a communist country? ("Notes on Reading the Soviet Work, *Political Economy*" [1961–1962].)

Our people can accomplish any achievement of imperialism and capitalism. I still do not believe that only the capitalists of Europe, North America, or Japan are capable of such achievements. ("Talk at the Reception for the Algerian Cultural Delegation" [April 15, 1964].)

From now on, the world must belong to the people, with the people of each country governing themselves; [it must] definitely not [be] a world where imperialism and its lackeys can continue to ride roughshod over others. ("Great Victories in Three Mass Movements" [October 23, 1951], in *SWM*, 5: 52.)

The contradictions in the world are basically the contradictions between socialism and imperialism. Under the pretexts of anti-Sovietism and anticommunism, imperialism has seized the Near East, Africa, and the Middle East. Of the two imperialist factions that contend for colonies, the greatest imperialist is the United States, followed by Britain and France. A wave of the national independence movement has now emerged in the colonies. The United States has resorted to force in Japan and Taiwan, while using both diplomacy and force in the Middle East. ("Summation at the Conference of Secretaries of Provincial and Municipal Committees" [January 1957].)

With the exception of Australia, the United States now wants to infringe on the other four of the five continents. ("Speech at the Supreme State Conference" [September 8, 1958].)

The Chinese people know that U.S. imperialism has repeatedly mistreated China and the whole world. They know, however, that only the ruling clique in the United States is bad, but the people of the United States are good. Even though many Americans are not yet awake, few of them are bad and the majority are good. ("Letter to Comrade Foster" [January 17, 1959].)

On the whole, the international situation is good. A few imperialist powers exist, but what of it? It wouldn't be terrifying even if there were several dozen more. ("Speech at the Second Plenum of the Eighth Central Committee of the Communist Party of China" [November 15, 1956], in *SWM*, 5: 318.)

Do not fear imperialism. It will not do if you are afraid; the more you fear, the weaker you are. Be prepared and fearless, and you will be

strong. ("Speech on the Consolidation of Military Work and the Cultivation of Revolutionary Successors" [June 16, 1964].)

The two major world powers, the United States and the Soviet Union,
befriend each other. They are attempting to control the whole world
between themselves. ("Talk at the Reception for Sasaki Kōzō, Kuroda
Hisao, and Hososako Kanemitsu of the Japan Socialist Party" [July 10,
1964].)

In recent months, the rightist opportunists have launched a wild assault, stating that nothing about the people's enterprise is good. All the
world's anti-Chinese and anticommunist elements together with the
bourgeois and petit bourgeois opportunist elements who have in the past
sneaked into the proletariat and the party of our country, have jointly
attacked us. Gosh, it seems as if they were trying to knock down the
K'un-lun mountains. Comrades, think about it. This handful of opportunists who wear the communist label within our country merely seize
on a few chicken feathers and onion skins as their banner to launch
attacks upon the party's general line, its Great Leap Forward, and its
people's communes. This is really like "huge ants shaking a giant tree;
their lack of self-knowledge is ludicrous and arrogant."[3] Since last year,
all the world's reactionaries have virtually cast a spell on us and smeared
our heads with dog blood. In my opinion, this is very good. If imperialism and its running dogs had not repeatedly cursed the great cause
of 650 million people, it would have been incomprehensible. The more
they curse us, the more pleased I shall be. Let them curse us for a half-
century, and we shall then see who is the winner and who is the loser.
("Letter to the Editor of the *Journal of Poetry*" [September 1, 1959].)

Imperialism colludes with, yet also contradicts, revisionism. There are
also contradictions among the revisionists. Revisionism prevails in fewer
than one hundred parties, but these parties are not very united. The
imperialists are also not very united. You can see that France and Britain
are not very united. ("Talk at the Reception for the Zanzibar Expert M.
M. Ali and His Wife" [June 18, 1964].)

The British are crafty and slippery, and the Americans are relatively
quick-tempered. The British often provide strategy and tactics. ("Talk
with the Directors of Various Cooperative Districts" [November 30,
1958].)

We should regard the struggle among the imperialists as a major
event. Lenin treated it as a great event, and so did Stalin. What they

called the revolutionary, indirect reservists referred to this [state of affairs]. In carrying out the revolution, China also received such assistance. In the past, contradictions existed in our country between the various landlord-comprador classes. Behind these contradictions lay contradictions among the various imperialists. Because of such inner contradictions, we fight directly only with some of our enemies at any given time, not with all of our enemies—as long as we can make good use of these contradictions. We also frequently gain time for rest. ("Notes on Reading the Soviet Work, *Political Economy*" [1961–1962].)

Great contradictions exist among the imperialists. If we utilize these contradictions, much work can be accomplished. This is a strategic policy. ("Summation at the Conference of Secretaries of Provincial and Municipal Committees" [January 1957].)

Much confusion prevails on the international scene. Disputes occur among the imperialists, and there is no peace in the world. Confusion emerges in France, Algeria, Latin America, Indonesia, Lebanon, and the rest of the capitalist world. We are concerned with all of these. Anything anti-imperialist is of benefit to us. ("Speech at the Second Session of the Eighth National Congress" [May 17, 1958].)

During the Middle East incident, a letter from the Soviet Union caused the United States to order an alert by the three branches of its armed forces. Who is afraid of whom? Both sides fear each other. Who is more afraid of whom? My belief is that imperialism fears us more. According to this estimation, if we sleep three successive nights, danger will arise. If worse comes to the worst, imperialism will become hysterical. ("Summation at the Conference of Secretaries of Provincial and Municipal Committees" [January 1957].)

The imperialists are really dispirited. They are decadent, confused, full of contradictions, and badly divided. They are ill at ease, and their good days are in the past. ("Speech at the Sixth Plenum of the Eighth Central Committee" [December 19, 1958].)

8. WAR AND PEACE

The reactionary forces of the world have already prepared for a third world war, and the danger of war exists. But the democratic forces of the people of the world greatly outnumber the reactionary forces and are forging ahead; they must and certainly can overcome the danger of war. ("Some Points in Appraisal of the Present International Situation" [April 1946], in *SWM*, 4: 1,181.)

The people's movement for peace and against war has gained ground in all countries. The national liberation movements to throw off the yoke of imperialism have greatly expanded; the emerging mass movements of the Japanese and German people against U.S. occupation and the growing people's liberation struggles of the oppressed nations in the East are especially noteworthy. ("Fight for a Fundamental Turn for the Better in the Nation's Financial and Economic Situation" [June 6, 1950], in *SWM*, 5: 15.)

The threat of war from the imperialist camp still exists, and so does the possibility of a third world war. (Ibid., in *SWM*, 5: 15.)

We are still encircled by imperialist forces, and we must be prepared for all possible contingencies. If the imperialists should unleash a war in the future, very likely they would launch a surprise attack as in World War II. ("Speeches at the National Conference of the Communist Party of China" [March 1955], in *SWM*, 5: 141.)

Just because we have won a victory, we must never relax our vigilance against frenzied plots for revenge by the imperialists and their running dogs. Whoever relaxes his vigilance disarms himself politically and falls into a passive position. ("Address to the Preparatory Committee of the New Political Consultative Conference" [June 15, 1949], in *SWM*, 4: 1,469.)

At present, the Soviet Union is no longer encircled by capitalism. This thought dangerously lulls people to sleep. Certainly the current situation differs greatly from that of the period when only one socialist country existed. West of the Soviet Union are the various socialist countries of Eastern Europe, and east of the Soviet Union are we [the Chinese] and the socialist countries of Korea and Vietnam. But guided missiles have no eyes, and they can strike a target from several to over ten thousand kilometers away. Around the entire socialist [camp] are scattered U.S. military bases, whose arrowheads all point toward the Soviet Union and the various socialist countries. Can it be said that the Soviet Union is no longer encircled by guided missiles? ("Notes on Reading the Soviet Work, *Political Economy*" [1961–1962].)

The danger of a world war and the threat to China come mainly from U.S. warmongers. They have occupied our Taiwan and the Taiwan Strait and are contemplating an atomic war. We have two principles: (1) we do not want war; and (2) we will strike back resolutely if invaded.

("The Chinese People Cannot Be Cowed by the Atom Bomb" [January 28, 1955], in *SWM*, 5: 136.)

World wars end not in favor of the warmongers but in favor of the communist parties and the revolutionary people in all lands. If the warmongers make war, then they must not blame us for making revolution or engaging in "subversive activities," as they keep saying all the time. (Ibid., in *SWM*, 5: 137.)

The seizure of power by armed force and the settlement of issues by war are respectively the central task and the highest form of revolution. This Marxist-Leninist principle of revolution universally holds for China and for all other countries.

But while the principle remains the same, its application by the party of the proletariat finds expression in varying ways according to varying conditions. Internally, capitalist countries practice bourgeois democracy (not feudalism) when they are not fascist or not at war; externally, they are not opposed by, but they themselves oppress, other nations. Therefore, the tasks of the party of the proletariat in capitalist countries are to educate the workers, strengthen itself through a long period of legal struggle, and thus prepare for the final overthrow of capitalism. In these countries, the question is one of a long legal struggle, of utilizing parliament as a platform, of economic and political strikes, and of organizing trade unions and educating the workers. There the form of organization is legal, and the form of struggle bloodless (nonbelligerent). On the issue of war, the communist parties in the capitalist countries oppose the imperialist wars waged by their own countries; if such wars occur, the policy of these parties is to bring about the defeat of the reactionary governments of their own countries. The one war the communist parties want to fight is the civil war for which they are preparing. But this insurrection and war should not be launched until the bourgeoisie becomes really helpless, until the majority of the proletariat is determined to rise in arms and fight, and until the rural masses are giving willing help to the proletariat. And when the time comes to launch such an insurrection, the first step will be to seize the cities and then advance into the countryside, not the other way around. All this has been done by communist parties in capitalist countries and has been proved correct by the October Revolution in Russia. ("Problems of War and Strategy" [November 6, 1938], in *SWM*, 2: 529–30.)

Every Communist must grasp the truth, "Political power grows out of the barrel of a gun." Our principle is that the party commands the gun, and the gun must never be allowed to command the party. Yet, having guns, we can create party organizations, as witness the powerful party organizations that the Eighth Route Army has created in northern China. We can also create cadres, create schools, create culture, create mass movements. Everything in Yenan has been created by having guns. All things grow out of the barrel of a gun. According to the Marxist theory of the state, the army is the chief component of state power. Whoever wants to seize and retain state power must have a strong army. Some people ridicule us as advocates of the "omnipotence of war." Yes, we advocate the omnipotence of revolutionary war; that is good, not bad—it is Marxist. (Ibid., in *SWM*, 2: 535.)

A great revolution can occur only through civil war. This is a rule. To see only the bad points and not the good points of war is a one-sided view of the problem of war. One-sided talk of the destructiveness of war is detrimental to the people's revolution. ("Notes on Reading the Soviet Work, *Political Economy*" [1961–1962].)

The communist party and revolutionary strength of every country must be prepared for two contingencies. One is to achieve victory through peaceful means, and the other is to gain political power by brute force; both are indispensable. General trends demonstrate that the bourgeoisie is unwilling to relinquish political power but wishes to fight. When the bourgeoisie is struggling for its life, why wouldn't it resort to force? The October Revolution and our revolution prepared for both contingencies. Before July 1917, Lenin sought to achieve victory through peaceful means. When the July incident revealed the impossibility of transferring political power into the hands of the proletariat, Lenin spent three months making military preparations and was thus able to gain victory in October. After the proletariat seized political power through the October Revolution, Lenin still wanted to use peaceful means, as well as the "hire and purchase" method, to liquidate capitalism and implement socialist reforms. But the bourgeoisie colluded with fourteen imperialist countries and launched counterrevolutionary armed uprisings and intervention. Only after three years of armed struggle under the leadership of the Russian party was the victory of the October Revolution consolidated. (Ibid.)

It will not be we who decide whether a world war breaks out. Even if a nonbelligerent agreement is signed, the possibilities of war still exist. When imperialism wishes to unleash a war, no agreement matters. Whether atom or hydrogen bombs will be used is another question.

Aside from the availability of chemical weapons, which are useless in war, conventional weapons will still be employed. Even if there is no war between the two camps, it cannot be guaranteed that there will be no war within the capitalist world. Imperialism can fight against imperialism; the bourgeoisie and the proletariat within an imperialist country can fight against each other; imperialism is fighting against colonies and semicolonies at present. War is a means of class conflicts. Only through war can classes be extinguished; only after the extinction of classes can war be permanently eliminated. If we do not carry on revolutionary wars, classes cannot become extinct. (Ibid.)

Daily we wish to relax [world] tension. Such a relaxation would benefit the world. But is tension detrimental to us? I don't think so. Tension is not totally harmful; it has its advantages. Why? Despite its harmful aspects, tension can mobilize men and horses, the backward strata of society, and the middle-of-the-road parties to wage struggles. If you fear atomic war, please consider the following. Beyond all my expectations, the bombardments at Quemoy and Ma-tsu have created a great storm and a huge cloud of smoke because people fear war and are afraid that the United States will create disasters everywhere. ("Speech at the Supreme State Conference" [September 5, 1958].)

During these last eight months, from August of last year [1958] to April of this year, two incidents have broken out, both of which have concerned us. One was the problem of Taiwan, and the other was that of Tibet. In August of last year there were great disturbances about Taiwan, as there now are about Tibet. In China, only these two places have not been [politically] reformed. Tibet, being part of the mainland, can be reached on wheels via highways. Unlike Taiwan, Tibet has not concluded a similar treaty with any other country; so our air force and army can be dispatched there. But Taiwan is different in nature, and it has concluded a treaty with the United States. Last year the Americans could not rest in peace in the Middle East, and the Middle East incident gave Eisenhower, Dulles, and many other Americans insomnia. Two days after the United Nations passed a resolution calling for the withdrawal of troops [from the Middle East], we began our bombardment [of Quemoy and Ma-tsu]. As soon as the [Middle East] trouble ended, trouble started here [in Taiwan], and the Americans came running scared.[4] The Americans immediately came from the Middle East to Taiwan pell-mell. Reinforcements were ordered from the U.S. West Coast, and a fleet was transferred to rendezvous in the Taiwan Strait. For a while, the United States did not know our intentions. Dulles subsequently stated that this was the largest rendezvous in their history. For example, in one location six out of the United States' twelve aircraft carriers were gathered. There were also many other naval ships. This huge rendezvous was based on their fear of our seizure of Quemoy, Ma-tsu and Taiwan. Chiang Kai-shek was so shaken that he was ready to move his home, and the Ministry of Economics actually moved to the countryside. Right after the August 23 bombardment, the United States decided to transfer its forces on the same day (or the next day). This was in August. Not until October was the United States able to see clearly, and it ordered an immediate withdrawal of its forces to the U.S. West Coast, Japan, and the Philippines. Because of the long distance and its late arrival, the Mediterranean contingent sailed to Manila for repairs before its hasty return to its home base. Among the consequences of this was the outcome of the U.S. election on November 4, in which the Republican party lost to the Democratic party. We did unpaid voluntary labor for the Democratic party. The Americans have always maltreated us. Before the Middle East incident, they published a memorandum stating that China was so mischievous that because of numerous allegations they would never grant us recognition. They also terminated the Geneva negotiations [over Sino-American relations]. Well, we gave them a deadline for negotiations. Later, at the conclusion of the Middle East incident, they did show up several days after our deadline. Our deadline was the fifteenth, and they responded on the seventeenth for negotiations. We did not publicize these events, for at that time we were not concerned with those affairs. We wished to resume the bombardment, and therefore I did not publicize the matter. ("Speech at the Sixteenth Session of the Supreme State Conference" [April 15, 1959].)

China wants peace. Whoever advocates peace has our support. We are not in favor of war. But we support the wars of oppressed peoples against imperialism. We support Cuba; we support the Algerian revolutionary war; we also support the war of the South Vietnamese people against U.S. imperialism. These revolutions are being waged by [the people] themselves. ("Talk at the Reception for the Chilean Newspaper Workers' Delegation" [June 23, 1964].)

American imperialism is even more isolated [now than before]. All the world's people know that imperialism is the chief warmonger. Imperialism is hated by all people, including those of the United States. The Soviet Union's imperialism is also clearly visible, especially in this

Middle East incident. The Soviet Union has again adopted Khrushchev's ways and dispatched more than 2,000 military experts to the United Arab Republic [Egypt]. At first it resorted to adventurism, sending naval vessels and persuading the United Arab Republic not to attack in advance. At the same time, it used the hot line to notify Johnson (Khrushchev did not have the hot line at his disposal). Subsequently Johnson told Israel to launch a sudden assault at once, which destroyed 60 percent of the United Arab Republic's aircraft on the ground. Of the total $2.3 billion in Soviet assistance to the United Arab Republic, $2 billion were lost, ending in the surrender of the United Arab Republic and the termination of the war. This was another grand exposé of the sellout of a national state. ("The Great Strategic Plan" [September 1967].)

9. OPPOSE THE POLICIES OF AGGRESSION AND WAR

If the American group of monopolistic capitalists insists on promoting its policies of aggression and war, it will some day be strangled to death by the people of the world. Other accomplices also will be so treated. ("Speech at the Supreme State Conference" [September 8, 1958].)

The history of aggression against China by U.S. imperialism, from 1840 when it helped the British in the Opium War to the time it was thrown out of China by the Chinese people, should be written into a concise textbook for the education of Chinese youth. (" 'Friendship' or Aggression?" [August 30, 1949], in SWM, 4: 1,509.)

For a long time, U.S. imperialism, more than any other imperialist country, emphasized activities in the sphere of spiritual aggression, ranging from religious to "philanthropic" and cultural undertakings. According to certain statistics, the investments of U.S. missionary and "philanthropic" organizations in China totaled U.S. $41.9 million; 14.7 percent of the assets of missionary organizations were in medical services, 38.2 percent in education, and 47.1 percent in religious activities. Many well-known educational institutions in China, such as Yenching University, Peking Union Medical College, the Huei Wen Academies, St. John's University, the University of Nanking, Soochow University, Hangchow Christian College, Hsiangya Medical School, West China Union University, and Lingnan University were established by Americans. It was in this field that Leighton Stuart made a name for himself;

this was how he became U.S. ambassador to China. Acheson and his like know what they are talking about, and his statement that "our friendship for that country has always been intensified by the religious, philanthropic, and cultural ties that have united the two peoples" has some foundation. It was all for the sake of "intensifying friendship," we are told, that the United States worked so hard and so deliberately at operating such undertakings for the 105 years following the signing of the treaty of 1844.

Participation in the eight-power allied expedition to defeat China in 1900, the extortion of the "Boxer indemnity," and the later use of this fund "for the education of Chinese students" for purposes of spiritual aggression—these too count as an expression of "friendship." (Ibid., in *SWM*, 4: 1,510.)

I have talked with Japanese friends. They say, "We feel very sorry that the imperial Japanese army invaded China." I reply, "No. If your imperial army had not invaded more than half of China, the Chinese people could not have been united to deal with you, and the Communist Party of China would not have been able to seize political power." ("Talk at the Reception for Sasaki Kōzō, Kuroda Hisao, and Hososako Kanemitsu of the Japan Socialist Party" [July 10, 1964].)

The Japanese tell me in Peking, "We are very ashamed of our past aggression." I say, "You have done a good deed. Precisely because of your aggression and occupation of over one-half of China, we became united and were able to lead the people of the entire country to expel you, and we are now in Peking." ("Speech at the Second Session of the Eighth National Congress" [May 17, 1958].)

Why do we wish to thank the imperial Japanese army? It was because of the advent of the imperial Japanese army that we fought against the imperial Japanese army and cooperated again with Chiang Kai-shek. After eight years of fighting, we expanded our military forces from 25,000 to 1,200,000 persons, with [revolutionary] bases having a population of 100,000,000. Don't you think that we should thank them? ("Talk at the Reception for Sasaki Kōzō, Kuroda Hisao, and Hososako Kanemitsu of the Japan Socialist Party" [July 10, 1964].)

In resisting aggressors, if there is no object, target, or opposing side, you cannot carry out resistance. Now that it [the U.S. aggressor] has come to stand on the opposite side and refused to go away, all the world's people are thus mobilized to oppose the U.S. aggressor. Generally speaking, its belated withdrawal appears to have brought not only harm but some benefits. Because of this, the people can tell it to hasten its departure and demand to know why it is not leaving. ("Speech at the Supreme State Conference" [September 5, 1958].)

All revolutionary forces within each country must unite, and the revolutionary forces of all countries must likewise unite, form an anti-imperialist united front headed by the Soviet Union, and follow correct policies; otherwise, victory will be impossible. ("Revolutionary Forces of the Whole World Unite, Fight Against Imperialist Aggression!" [November 1948], in *SWM*, 4: 1,361.)

I think that the American people and the peoples of all countries menaced by U.S. aggression should unite and struggle against the attacks of U.S. reactionaries and their running dogs in these countries. Only by victory in this struggle can a third world war be avoided; otherwise it is inevitable. ("Talk with the American Correspondent Anna Louise Strong" [August 1946], in *SWM*, 4: 1,192.)

Japan is anti-American. Not only the Communist Party of Japan and the Japanese people but also the big capitalists are anti-American. ("Summary of a Talk at the Spring Festival" [February 13, 1964].)

The United States calls us an "aggressor," and we call it an aggressor. It calls us "belligerent elements," and we call the big capitalists of the U.S. government belligerent elements. ("Talk at the Reception for the Chilean Newspaper Workers' Delegation" [June 23, 1964].)

The Americans have reached out their hands into our entire western Pacific Ocean and Southeast Asia; they have overreached themselves. The Seventh Fleet is the largest fleet of the United States, [a country] which has twelve aircraft carriers; half of those belong to the Seventh Fleet—six carriers. It has another fleet—the Sixth Fleet—in the Mediterranean Sea. When we bombarded Quemoy in 1958, the Americans became nervous and transferred part of the Third Fleet [*sic*] eastward [in August]. The Americans control Europe, Canada, and all of Latin America except Cuba. Now they have penetrated Africa and are fighting in the Congo. ("Talk at the Reception for Sasaki Kōzō, Kuroda Hisao, and Hososako Kanemitsu of the Japan Socialist Party" [July 10, 1964].)

U.S. imperialism has formed military organizations like NATO, and [the] Bagdad and Manila [Pacts]. What is the nature of these organizations? We say that they are aggressive. Is it really true that they are aggressive? But at what side does their spearhead point? Does it aim to attack socialism or nationalism? In my view, its aim is to attack nationalism, that is, Egypt, Lebanon, and the weak countries in the Middle East. It will not assault the socialist countries, unless Hungary fails, Poland, Czechoslovakia, and East Germany collapse, the Soviet Union experiences problems, and we also are afflicted with serious problems. ("Speech at the Supreme State Conference" [September 5, 1958].)

People of all countries in the socialist camp, unite; people of all countries in Asia, Africa, and Latin America, unite; people of all continents in the whole world, unite; all peace-loving countries, unite; all those countries that have been invaded, controlled, suffered intervention, and been maltreated by the United States, unite. [We] must form the broadest [possible] united front, oppose the warmongering and aggressive policies of U.S. imperialism, and safeguard world peace. ("Talk in Support of the Panamanian People's Anti-U.S., Patriotic, and Just Struggle" [January 12, 1964].)

10. RESISTING U.S. AGGRESSION AND AIDING KOREA

The focus of U.S. strategy is Europe. They did not anticipate that we would send volunteers to aid Korea when they dispatched forces to invade it. ("Let Us Unite and Clearly Distinguish Between Ourselves and the Enemy" [August 4, 1952], in *SWM*, 5: 68.)

In order to support the Korean people's war of liberation and to resist the attacks of U.S. imperialism and its running dogs, thereby safeguarding the interests of the people of Korea, China, and all other countries in the East, I hereby order the Chinese People's Volunteers to march speedily to Korea and join the Korean comrades in fighting the aggressors and winning a glorious victory. ("Order to the Chinese People's Volunteers" [October 8, 1950], in *SWM*, 5: 32.)

In the movement to resist U.S. aggression and aid Korea, the Chinese people are more broadly united than ever before and are waging a determined struggle against the U.S. imperialist forces of aggression. Embodying the mighty will of the Chinese people, the Chinese People's Volunteers have joined forces with the Korean People's Army in smashing U.S. imperialism's mad scheme to overrun and occupy the Democratic People's Republic of Korea and then invade the Chinese mainland; thus, the peace-loving peoples of Korea, China, Asia, and the world have been inspired and made more confident in their defense of peace and resistance to aggression. ("Great Victories in Three Mass Movements" [October 23, 1951], in *SWM*, 5: 48–49.)

[We] Chinese and Korean comrades should unite as closely as brothers, go through thick and thin together, stick together in life and death, and fight to the end to defeat our common enemy. [We] Chinese comrades must consider Korea's cause as our own; and the comrades and fighters must be instructed to cherish every hill, every river, every tree, and every blade of grass in Korea and to take not a single needle or a single thread from the Korean people, just as we feel about our own country and treat our own people. This is the political basis for winning victory. As long as we act this way, final victory will be assured. ("The Chinese People's Volunteers Should Cherish Every Hill, Every River, Every Tree, and Every Blade of Grass in Korea" [January 19, 1951], in *SWM*, 5: 33.)

To what was this victory due? Just now, fellow members attributed it to correct leadership. Leadership is one factor; nothing can succeed without correct leadership. But we won mainly because ours was a people's war; the whole nation supported it, and the peoples of China and Korea fought shoulder to shoulder. ("Our Great Victory in the War to Resist U.S. Aggression and Aid Korea and Our Future Tasks" [September 12, 1953], in *SWM*, 5: 101.)

The problem of our ability to fight [in Korea] was solved within the first two to three months. The enemy had more artillery, but its morale was low; it was rich in metal but poor in morale.

The problem of our ability to hold out was also solved last year. Our solution was to dig tunnels. We constructed two tiers of defense works. When the enemy attacked, we got into the tunnels. Sometimes the enemy occupied positions overhead, but what lay below remained in our hands. When they occupied our positions, we counterattacked, inflicting heavy casualties on them. We used this homespun method to collect foreign guns. The enemy was entirely at a loss as to how to cope with us.

It was quite some time before the problem of food supplies, that is, the problem of ensuring provisions, was solved. At first we did not know that grain could be stored in tunnels. Now we know. Each division has grain reserves for three months, its own storage area, and a meeting hall to boot, and our men are making a go of life in the tunnels. ("Let Us Unite and Clearly Distinguish Between Ourselves and the Enemy" [August 4, 1952], in *SWM*, 5: 67.)

Each belligerent called its own battle line a bastion of iron. Ours was truly a bastion of iron. Our soldiers and cadres were resourceful and brave and dared to look death in the face. In contrast, the U.S. aggressor troops were afraid of death, and their officers were somewhat rigid and rather inflexible. Their battle line was not solid and was anything but a bastion of iron. ("Our Great Victory in the War to Resist U.S. Aggression and Aid Korea and Our Future Tasks" [September 12, 1953], in *SWM*, 5: 101–2.)

We grew stronger and stronger through fighting. The Americans failed to undermine our positions; on the contrary, their units were always wiped out by us. (Ibid., in *SWM*, 5: 102.)

We want peace. But as long as U.S. imperialism does not give up its savage and unreasonable demands and the plot to enlarge its aggression, the Chinese people are determined to join with the Korean people and to continue to fight. This is not because we are bellicose. We are willing to cease fire immediately and leave the remaining questions to be solved in the future. But U.S. imperialism is unwilling to do so. Well, we shall continue to fight. No matter how long U.S. imperialism is willing to fight, we are prepared to continue fighting against it—until U.S. imperialism is willing to stop or the Chinese and Korean peoples have achieved complete victory. ("Speech at the Fourth Session of the First National Committee of the Chinese People's Political Consultative Conference" [February 7, 1953].)

Just how long will the fighting go on, and just when will the negotiations draw to a close? I say the negotiations will continue, the fighting will go on, but there will be a truce.

Why? A thirty years war or a hundred years war is highly improbable because a long war is contrary to interests of the United States. ("Let Us Unite and Clearly Distinguish Between Ourselves and the Enemy" [August 4, 1952], in *SWM*, 5: 67.)

Eventually the imperialist and capitalist systems will turn out like this: they will eventually be replaced by the socialist system. The ideologies [of imperialism and capitalism] are alike. Dialectical materialism must displace idealism; atheism must replace religion. This is based on the viewpoint of strategy. This strategy differs from that of the tactical stage, which allows compromises. On the 38° line in Korea, did we not compromise with the Americans? In Vietnam, did we not compromise with the French? ("Speech on the Methods of Solidarity" [August 1964].)

The U.S. imperialists were very arrogant; if at all possible, they always refused to talk reason and did so after a fashion only when driven into a tight corner. ("Our Great Victory in the War to Resist U.S. Aggression and Aid Korea and Our Future Tasks" [September 12, 1953], in *SWM*, 5: 102.)

One important reason for the consolidation of the victory of the October Revolution was the multiplicity of internal contradictions within imperialism. Then fourteen countries intervened, but none sent many troops, and they were disunited and competed with one another. In the Korean War, the United States and its allies were not united and did not exert themselves in war. Not only was the United States indecisive, but also Britain and France were unwilling [to fight]. ("Notes on Reading the Soviet Work, *Political Economy*" [1961–1962].)

For more than two decades we fought without an air force, and we were always on the receiving end of enemy bombing. Now we have an air force and antiaircraft guns of our own as well as artillery and tanks. The war to resist U.S. aggression and aid Korea is an important school for large-scale military exercises; such exercises are better than a military academy. ("Let Us Unite and Clearly Distinguish Between Ourselves and the Enemy" [August 4, 1952], in *SWM*, 5: 66–67.)

There are people who have been slaves too long and feel inferior in everything and don't stand up straight in the presence of foreigners. They are just like Chia Kuei[5] in the opera *The Famen Temple*, who, when asked to take a seat, refuses to do so, giving the excuse that he is used to standing in attendance. Here we need to bestir ourselves, enhance our national confidence, and encourage the spirit typified by [the slogan] "Scorn U.S. imperialism," which was promoted during the movement to resist U.S. aggression and aid Korea. ("On the Ten Major Relationships" [April 25, 1956], in *SWM*, 5: 287.)

The imperialist aggressors ought to remember that the Chinese people are now organized, they are not to be trifled with. Once they are provoked to anger, they can make things get very tough. ("Our Great Victory in the War to Resist U.S. Aggression and Aid Korea and Our Future Tasks" [September 12, 1953], in *SWM*, 5: 103.)

We are for peace but are not afraid of war; we are ready for both. We have the support of the people. In the war to resist U.S. aggression and aid Korea, people fell over each other to enlist. The conditions for enlistment were stiff; only one in a hundred was chosen. People said that the conditions were stricter than those for choosing a husband for one's daughter. If U.S. imperialism wants to resume the fighting, we will take it on again. (Ibid., in *SWM*, 5: 104.)

If you have never taken someone on, you are liable to be scared of him. We fought them [the United States] for 33 months and got to know them for what they are worth. American imperialism is not terrifying; it is nothing to make a fuss about. Such is our experience; indeed it is an invaluable piece of experience. (Ibid., in *SWM*, 5: 103.)

Imperialism calls us "aggressors" and "bellicose elements." In a certain way, this is correct because of our support of Castro, Ben Bella, and the war of the people of South Vietnam against the United States. Moreover, in 1950–1953, the United States invaded Korea, and we supported the war of the Korean people against U.S. imperialism. This policy of ours has been openly declared, and we shall never give it up. We must support the war of the people of all countries against imperialism. If we don't, we shall be committing a mistake and not be communists. ("Talk at the Reception for the Chilean Newspapers Workers' Delegation" [June 23, 1964].)

11. THE THIRD WORLD

Today things are entirely different; the great People's Republic of China has been founded, the people's democracies have been established, the level of political consciousness of the people of the world has been raised, the struggle for national liberation has surged throughout Asia and North Africa, the strength of the imperialist bloc as a whole has been profoundly weakened, and, what is of vital importance, the strength of the Soviet Union, our closest ally, has been greatly enhanced. ("Great Victories in Three Mass Movements" [October 23, 1951], in *SWM*, 5: 52.)

I think that the Americans are afraid of fighting; we also fear fighting. The question is who is more afraid. This is a viewpoint, as well as an observation. Please use this viewpoint to take a look at and observe carefully the next one, two, three, four, and more years. Is the West more afraid of the East, or is the East more afraid of the West? According to my reckoning, Dulles fears us a little more; and Western countries like Britain, the United States, Germany, and France are a little more afraid of us [than we are of them]. Why do they fear us a little more? It is a question of strength and opinion. Opinion is strength. The population on our side is more numerous, and the one on their side less so. Among communism, nationalism, and imperialism, communism is closer to nationalism. But nationalism occupies a relatively large area, namely, three continents—Asia, Africa, and Latin America. Even though these continents contain many pro-Western rulers, such as those in Thailand, Pakistan, Japan, Turkey, and Iran, there are probably more pro-Easterners among the people. Only the monopolistic capitalists and those who have been most severely drugged by them advocate war. For instance, the rulers in several northern European countries are capitalists, but they are unwilling to wage war. Such are relative strengths [of communism and capitalism]. ("Speech at the Supreme State Conference" [September 5, 1958].)

Lenin said: "The more backward the country, the more difficult is its transition from capitalism to socialism." This statement now seems incorrect. In reality, the more backward the economy, the easier is its transition from capitalism to socialism, not the more difficult. The poorer the people, the more revolutionary they are. Because the number of employed people in the Western capitalist countries is greater, the level of wages is higher, and the laborers are very deeply influenced by the bourgeoisie. It is therefore not so easy to carry out socialist reforms in these countries. The degree of mechanization in these countries is very high; after the success of the revolution, the problem of further raising the degree of mechanization is not great. The important problem lies in the reform of the people. In the East, such countries as Russia and China were originally backward and poor, but now the socialist system is not only more advanced than in the West, the growth rate of productivity is also higher than in the West. Even the history of development of various capitalist countries shows that backward countries overtake the advanced. For example, the United States overtook Britain at the end of the nineteenth century, and Germany overtook Britain at the beginning of the twentieth century. ("Notes on Reading the Soviet Work, *Political Economy*" [1961–1962].)

The situation in these three continents—Asia, Africa, and Latin America—is revolutionary, and they constitute the majority of the world's population by far. This is a fact. These constitute the majority of the world, while Europe, New Zealand, Australia, and North America constitute the minority. ("Talk at the Reception for the Zanzibar Expert M. M. Ali and His Wife" [June 18, 1964].)

If there is to be a revolution, there must be a revolutionary party. Without a revolutionary party, without a party based on the Marxist-Leninist revolutionary theory and in the Marxist-Leninist revolutionary style, it is impossible to lead the working class and the broad masses of the people to defeat imperialism and its running dogs. ("Revolutionary Forces of the Whole World Unite, Fight Against Imperialist Aggression!" [November 1948], in *SWM*, 4: 1,360.)

Vast numbers of the people of India and China are friendly to each other. I believe that vast numbers of people in India are also friendly to the people of Japan, except that the Indian government is controlled and influenced by imperialism and revisionism to a great extent. Three countries assisted India with arms to attack us: the United States, Britain, and the Soviet Union. ("Talk at the Reception for Sasaki Kōzō, Kuroda Hisao, and Hososako Kanemitsu of the Japan Socialist Party" [July 10, 1964].)

In the Congo (I refer to the Greater Congo), there was Lumumba, a national hero, who was murdered, but the struggle is still expanding. ("Talk at the Reception for the Zanzibar Expert M. M. Ali and His Wife" [June 18, 1964].)

Since the overthrow of the Farouk dynasty in 1952 by the Egyptians, changes in Africa have been extensive. Discontented with their defeats, the British and French carried out assaults on the Suez Canal. In another place, Algeria, war was waged for eight years. With a small number of troops, Algeria defeated several hundred thousand French forces. In consequence, French imperialism was defeated, and Algeria achieved victory. (Ibid.)

Our friends in Latin America, Asia, and Africa are in the same position as we and are doing the same kind of work, namely, doing something for the people to lessen imperialist oppression of them. If we do a good job, we can root out imperialist oppression. In this we are comrades. ("American Imperialism Is a Paper Tiger" [July 14, 1956], in *SWM*, 5: 292.)

Great improvements are now occurring in Latin America. Vice-president Nixon was not welcome in eight countries and was spat on and stoned. As the United States' political representative, he was greeted with spitting by these people. This was done to slight his "dignity" and to disregard "courtesies": he did not count in their minds. [Their thought was] you are our opponent; let us greet you with spitting and rocks. ("Speech at the Supreme State Conference" [September 5, 1958].)

Brazil is a big country, with 60 million people and an area as large as that of China. Brazil has always been oppressed by U.S. imperialism. ("Directive at the Symposium for a Few Delegates to the First Session of the Committee of the Second National Industry and Commerce Association Conference" [December 8, 1956].)

U.S. imperialism massacres foreigners, as well as the white and black people of its own country. Nixon's fascist, tyrannical conduct has lit the ardent fire of the U.S. revolutionary mass movement. The Chinese people are determined to render assistance to the revolutionary struggle of the American people. I believe that the valiantly fighting American people will eventually achieve victory, and the U.S. fascist reign will certainly encounter disaster. ("People of the Whole World Unite, Defeat the U.S. Aggressors and All Their Running Dogs" [May 20, 1970].)

Although the Communist Party of the United States temporarily finds itself in an unfavorable position, your struggle is very significant and will certainly bear abundant and durable fruits. The dark night will end. Since the U.S. reactionary forces have already run up against a wall and show signs of moribundity, the current strength of the enemy and the weakness of our side in the United States is only a temporary phenomenon. It will definitely change to the contrary. ("Letter to Comrade Foster" [January 17, 1959].)

To start a war, the U.S. reactionaries must first attack the American people. They are already attacking the American people—oppressing the workers and democratic circles in the United States politically and economically and preparing to impose fascism there. The people of the United States should rise up and resist the attacks of the U.S. reactionaries. I believe that they will. ("Talk with the American Correspondent Anna Louise Strong" [August 1946], in *SWM*, 4: 1,191.)

The goal of the North Atlantic Treaty Organization is to attack nationalism and indigenous communism in its member states (concentrating on attacking the intermediate zone—Asia, Africa, and Latin America). It has been defensive toward the socialist camp, except for the Hungarian incident. But in [our] propaganda we say on the contrary that its purpose is to launch an attack [on socialism]. Do not be misled by our own propaganda. ("Talk with the Directors of Various Cooperative Districts" [November 30, 1958].)

"Lift a rock and hit one's own foot" is a Chinese proverb used to describe the conduct of certain foolish persons. The reactionaries in various countries rank among such foolish persons. Their many varieties of oppression of the revolutionary people can, in the end, only incite people to wage a more extensive and more violent revolution. ("Speech at the U.S.S.R. Supreme Soviet Meeting in Celebration of the 40th Anniversary of the October Socialist Revolution" [November 6, 1957].)

The people of all of Asia, Africa, and Latin America are anti-U.S. imperialism. Many people in Europe, North America, and Oceania are also anti-(U.S.) imperialism. Some imperialists are also anti-(U.S.) imperialism. De Gaulle's anti-Americanism is further evidence of this. Now we put forward the following viewpoint: There are two intermediate zones: Asia, Africa, and Latin America constitute the first intermediate zone; Europe, North America, and Oceania constitute the second intermediate zone. Japanese monopolistic capitalism also belongs to the second intermediate zone. Although you [the Japan Socialist party] oppose your own monopolistic capitalism, they [the Japanese capitalists] are also dissatisfied with the United States. At present, some of these people openly oppose the United States. Others are dependent on the United States. In my view, many of these people will in the future drive away the Americans who ride herd on them because Japan is really a great nation. It dared to fight the United States, Britain, and France; it bombarded Pearl Harbor and occupied the Philippines, Vietnam, Thailand, Burma, Malaya, and Indonesia; it struck at the eastern part of India but withdrew and suffered defeat because of too many mosquitoes and typhoons during the summer there. Japan lost 200,000 soldiers. I do not believe that this kind of monopolistic capitalism will let U.S. imperialism easily ride herd on it. I am not supporting another bombardment of Pearl Harbor or the [re-]occupation of the Philippines, Vietnam, Thailand, Burma, Indonesia, and Malaya. Certainly, I do not support another attack on Korea and China. Wouldn't it be good if Japan achieves complete independence and establishes friendly relations, as well as solves its economic problems, on a mutual and fraternal basis with all of Asia, Africa, Latin America, and those people in Europe who are willing to oppose U.S. imperialism? ("Talk at the Reception for Sasaki Kōzō, Kuroda Hisao, and Hososako Kanemitsu of the Japan Socialist Party" [July 10, 1964].)

We must actively support the national independence and liberation movements of various countries in Asia, Africa, and Latin America, as well as the peace movements and just struggles of all countries in the world. ("Opening Address at the Eighth National Congress of the Communist Party of China" [September 15, 1956].)

12. AMERICAN IMPERIALISM IS A PAPER TIGER

American imperialism seems to be a huge, monstrous thing, but it is really a paper tiger in its death throes. ("People of the Whole World Unite, Defeat the U.S. Aggressors and All Their Running Dogs" [May 20, 1970].)

American imperialism is a very ferocious imperialism and the biggest imperialism. ("Talk at the Reception for the Zanzibar Expert M. M. Ali and His Wife" [June 18, 1964].)

Now American imperialism is quite strong, but its strength is not real. It is very weak politically because it is divorced from the masses of the people and is disliked by everyone—including the American people. In appearance it is very powerful, but in reality it is nothing to fear; it is a paper tiger. Outwardly a tiger, it is made of paper, unable to withstand the wind and the rain. I believe the United States is nothing but a paper tiger. ("American Imperialism Is a Paper Tiger" [July 14, 1956], in SWM, 5: 291.)

When we say American imperialism is a paper tiger, we are speaking in terms of strategy. Regarding it as a whole, we must belittle it. But regarding each part, we must take it seriously. It has claws and fangs, and we must destroy it piecemeal. For instance, if it has ten fangs, knock off one the first time, and there will be nine left; knock off another, and there will be eight left. When all the fangs are gone, it will still have claws. If we deal with it earnestly step by step, we will certainly succeed in the end.

Strategically, we must utterly belittle American imperialism. Tactically, we must take it seriously. In struggling against it, we must take each battle, each encounter, seriously. At present, the United States is powerful, but when looked at in a broader perspective, as a whole, and from a long-term viewpoint, it has no popular support and its policies are disliked by the people because it oppresses and exploits them. For this reason, the tiger is doomed. (Ibid., in SWM, 5: 291–92.)

The United States is beholden everywhere. It is beholden not only to the countries of Latin America, Asia, and Africa, but also to the countries of Europe and Oceania. The whole world, Britain included, dislikes the United States. (Ibid., in SWM, 5: 289.)

None of the countries in the East is free from U.S. aggression. The United States has invaded China's Taiwan province, Japan, Korea, the Philippines, Vietnam, and Pakistan—all suffer from U.S. aggression, although some of them are allies of the United States. (Ibid., in *SWM*, 5: 289.)

Everything is subject to change. The big, decadent forces will give way to the small, newborn forces. The small forces will grow into big forces because the majority of the people demands this change. The imperialist forces of the United States will decrease in size because the American people, too, are dissatisfied with their government. (Ibid., in *SWM*, 5: 289.)

The countries of America, Asia, and Africa seemingly must continue quarreling with the United States till the very end, till the paper tiger is destroyed by the wind and the rain. (Ibid., in *SWM*, 5: 292.)

All reactionaries are paper tigers. In appearance, reactionaries are terrifying, but in reality they are not so powerful. From a long-term point of view, it is not the reactionaries but the people who are really powerful. In Russia, before the February Revolution in 1917, which side was really strong? On the surface the czar was strong, but he was swept away by a single gust of wind in the February Revolution. In the final analysis, the strength in Russia lay on the side of the soviets of workers, peasants, and soldiers. The czar was just a paper tiger. Wasn't Hitler once considered formidable? But history proved that he was a paper tiger. So was Mussolini; so was Japanese imperialism. In contrast, the strength of the Soviet Union and of the people in all countries who loved democracy and freedom proved much greater than had been foreseen. ("Talk with the American Correspondent Anna Louise Strong" [August 1946], in *SWM*, 4: 1,193.)

American imperialism is lawless and seeks hegemony everywhere. It has placed itself in the position of being an enemy to the people of the entire world and has consequently become increasingly isolated. The atom and hydrogen bombs of American imperialism do not frighten anyone who is unwilling to be a slave, and the surging indignation of the world's people against American imperialism is insurmountable. The victory of the world's people over American imperialism and its running dogs will certainly be even greater. ("Talk in Support of the Panamanian People's Anti-U.S., Patriotic, and Just Struggle" [January 12, 1964].)

The atom bomb is a paper tiger that American reactionaries use to scare people. It looks terrible, but in fact it isn't. Of course, the atom bomb is a weapon of mass slaughter, but the outcome of a war is decided by the people, not by one or two new types of weapons. ("Talk with the

American Correspondent Anna Louise Strong" [August 1946], in *SWM*, 4: 1,192.)

In my opinion, all reactionaries who are said to be strong are merely paper tigers because they are alienated from the people. Beware! Wasn't Hitler a paper tiger? Wasn't Hitler defeated? I say that the czar was also a paper tiger, the Chinese emperor was a paper tiger, and Japanese imperialism was a paper tiger. You see that all were overthrown. American imperialism has not been defeated, and it still has its atom bombs. In my view, it will be overthrown, and it, too, is a paper tiger. ("Speech at the Moscow Conference of the Communist and Socialist Parties of Various Countries" [November 18, 1957].)

We have always regarded American imperialism as a paper tiger. Unfortunately, there is only one American imperialism; we would not mind if there were ten more, for all of them would perish sooner or later. ("Speech at the Second Session of the Eighth Central Committee" [May 17, 1958].)

We are a little afraid of the United States because the United States is our enemy. The United States is a little afraid of us, which shows that we are an an enemy, and a powerful enemy as well, of the United States. In science and technology we should observe security measures lest our secrets be stolen. ("Talk on Sakada's Writings" [August 24, 1964].)

We have experienced many problems in the course of our development, but remember that foreign countries also experience problems. For example, the United States has its problems. . . . The United States finds it difficult to manage its own affairs. In my view, economic crises will appear in that country and in Britain, France, Western Europe, the Free World, the Western world, and [all] the Western countries. The internal contradictions [in these countries] are tremendous; economic crises are inevitable and unavoidable. The U.S. moon is not necessarily better; this must still be proven. From time to time, the United States possesses a few more atom bombs and more catties of iron and steel. Right now it looks powerful. Do we recognize this point? We do. The people do not understand us when we disparage the United States as a paper tiger since it possesses so much. We call it a paper tiger because it is built on an unstable foundation. Whose foundation is stabler? Our foundation is stabler, and so is the foundation of socialism. The socialist camp is not entirely stable, and we also have defects and shortcomings. Our people are dissatisfied with us in many ways, and our economy and culture are backward. The entire socialist [camp] is more backward than the United States, but the latter is built on a more contradictory basis. Do not forget this point. ("Closing Remarks at the Supreme State Conference" [March 2, 1957].)

Imperialism brandishes its atom bombs and its hydrogen bombs to scare us, but they don't frighten us either. The world is so constituted that there is always one thing to conquer another. When one thing is used in attack, there is bound to be another thing to conquer it. If you have read the novel *Apotheosis of Heroes*,[6] you will know that there is no such thing as an invincible "magic weapon." ("Speeches at the National Conference of the Communist Party of China" [March 1955], in *SWM*, 5: 153.)

13. THE PEOPLE'S WAR

The danger of a world war and the threat to China come mainly from U.S. warmongers. They have occupied our Taiwan and the Taiwan Strait and are contemplating an atomic war. We have two principles: (1) we do not want war; (2) we will strike back resolutely if invaded. This is what we teach members of the Communist party and the whole nation. The Chinese people cannot be cowed by U.S. atomic blackmail. Our country has a population of 600 million and an area of 9.6 million square kilometers. The United States cannot annihilate the Chinese nation with its small stack of atom bombs. Even if American atom bombs were so powerful that when dropped on China they would make a hole through the earth or even blow it up, that would mean little to the universe as a whole, although it might be a major event for the solar system. ("The Chinese People Cannot Be Cowed by the Atom Bomb" [January 28, 1955], in *SWM*, 5: 136–37.)

We have an old expression, "millet plus rifles." In the case of the United States, it is planes plus atom bombs. However, if the United States with its planes plus atom bombs launched a war of aggression against China, then China with its millet plus rifles would surely emerge the victor. (Ibid., in *SWM*, 5: 137.)

Our national defense will be consolidated, and no imperialists will ever again be allowed to invade our land. Our people's armed forces must be maintained and developed on the foundation of the heroic and steeled People's Liberation Army. We will have not only a powerful army but also a powerful air force and a powerful navy. ("The Chinese People Have Stood Up!" [September 21, 1949], in *SWM*, 5: 6.)

Imperialists have bullied us so much that we must deal with them seriously. We not only need a powerful regular army, but we must also establish a large militia. In this way, if imperialism invades our country, it will have difficulty moving even an inch. ("Talk with a New China News Agency Correspondent" [September 29, 1958].)

Because a monopolistic bourgeoisie exists in the world and its members may recklessly make trouble anywhere, we must be prepared to fight. This matter must be clarified among the cadres. First, we do not want to fight and we oppose fighting; so does the Soviet Union. We fight only if they attack first and force us to fight. Second, we do not fear fighting, and we are ready to fight when necessary. At present we have only grenades and homemade bombs. Hydrogen and atom bomb warfare is certainly horrible and kills people. For this reason, we oppose fighting. But the decision [to go to war] is not in our hands. If imperialism wants to fight, we must be prepared for all exigencies and fight if necessary. In a word, even if half of our people are killed, that is nothing to be feared. This [estimate] is an exaggeration. From the viewpoint of the entire history of the universe, I do not believe that there is anything to be so pessimistic about. ("Speech at the Supreme State Conference" [September 5, 1958].)

We fought against India for several weeks. Why did we later withdraw our troops? Because their soldiers had all scattered and none remained, and we had no adversary to fight! Now we have withdrawn to twenty kilometers behind the boundary. The Indians have now improved and behave themselves. ("Talk at the Reception for the Nepalese Educational Delegation" [August 29, 1964].)

No matter where the enemy comes from, we must be prepared. Our country will never perish. Each level of the party committees must attend to military and militia work. . . . In a country like ours with an extensive battlefront, can we entrust [national defense] to several million Liberation Army soldiers of the central authorities alone? Since we cannot, each of us must plan to assume responsibility for guarding our territories. . . . Let them strike with atom bombs if they wish! When they drop an atom bomb, we'll depart. When they enter a city, we'll also enter. Our enemies will not dare to drop atom bombs. We'll wage door-to-door fighting and struggle against them. ("Speech on the Consolidation of

Military Work and the Cultivation of Revolutionary Successors" [June 16, 1964].)

Military affairs are learned from practice. Thus, do not regard Marxism and philosophy as mysteries. ("Speech at the Hangchow Conference" [May 1963].)

Do not wage battles without preparation. If materiel is not ready and soldiers are not well trained, do not fight. ("Directive on the Socialist Education Movement" [May 1963].)

We must also take fighting into our considerations. We must have strategic plans. It is unacceptable for the party committees in any location to control only civilian affairs and money but not military affairs and guns. As long as imperialism exists, the danger of war remains. ("Speech on the Third Five-Year Plan" [June 6, 1964].)

In fighting we must rely on China as a prop; relying on revisionism is useless. If an enemy breaks in, we can fight our way out. Generally speaking, we are prepared to fight, to wage battles intrepidly, and to deal with atom bombs coolly. Fear not. The worst that can happen is universal confusion and the death of some. Everyone must die, whether standing up or lying down. Carry on if alive, and half our people will survive even if the other half die. ("Speech on the Consolidation of Military Work and the Cultivation of Revolutionary Successors" [June 16, 1964].)

I hear that U.S. troops use our materials to teach the reactionary troops in South Vietnam to attack the Vietnamese people. Since our experience is based on the fighting experience of a people's army, as well as the experience accumulated by a people's army, they can never utilize it. ("Talk at the Reception for the Algerian Cultural Delegation" [April 15, 1964].)

People of the whole world, unite; defeat the U.S. aggressors and all their running dogs! People of the whole world, have courage, dare to fight, fear no difficulties, and follow one after another. Then the whole world will belong to the people. All devils will be exterminated. ("Statement in Support of the Congolese [Leopoldville] People's Opposition to U.S. Aggression" [November 28, 1964].)

Pursuing the Proletarian Revolutionary Line or the Rightist Capitulationist Line?

(The People's Press, Shanghai, June 1977)

DOCUMENT THREE

 The great leader and teacher, Chairman Mao, instructed us: "All affairs in the world are complicated and determined by various factors. Look at a problem from various viewpoints, not from a single viewpoint."

The counterrevolutionary, double-faced clique, which includes renegades, secret agents, and incorrigible capitalist roaders, belongs to the same counterrevolutionary, revisionist system made up of Ch'en Tu-hsiu, Ch'ü Ch'iu-pai, Li Li-san, Lo Chang-lung, Wang Ming, Chang Kuo-t'ao, Kao Kang, Jao Sou-shih, P'eng Te-huai, Liu Shao-ch'i, Lin Piao, and Teng Hsiao-p'ing. They have adopted the counterrevolutionary methods of always using pseudorevolution to oppose revolution, employing their pseudorevolutionary side to conceal their counterrevolutionary side, and utilizing legality to conceal illegality. The banner they raise is the Communist party emblem; the goods they sell are antiparty contraband. While proclaiming the Thought of Mao Tse-tung, they indulge in criminal acts against the party, against socialism, and against the Thought of Mao Tse-tung. If we look at problems from only a single viewpoint, we shall certainly be deluded.

On September 9, 1976, after the great leader and teacher, Chairman Mao, passed away, the Central Committee of the party, the Standing Committee of the National People's Congress, the State Council, and the Military Commission of the Central Committee of the party published the "Message to the Whole Party, the Whole Army, and the People of All Nationalities Throughout the Country," which solemnly declared: "We must continue the behest bequeathed by Chairman Mao, persist in taking the class struggle as the key link, keep to the party's basic line, and persevere in continuing the revolution under the dictatorship of the proletariat."

With regard to the line and policies enunciated in the "Message to the Whole Party, the Whole Army, and the People of All Nationalities Throughout the Country" by the party's Central Committee after the death of Chairman Mao, there can be no doubt that we should pursue them with full vigor. But among our comrades are some who have already forgotten them and voluntarily drifted endlessly with the tide. Some people have even taken up the mantle of Liu Shao-ch'i and Lin Piao. After appropriating our revolutionary slogans, they have persistently manipulated these slogans in order to confound right and wrong and black and white and to create ideological confusion for the purpose of misleading the masses. In the light of events since the death of Chairman Mao ten months ago can we say whether our party is really pursuing the proletarian revolutionary line or the rightist capitulationist line? This question has become so serious that the time has come to use the ideological weapon of Marxism to clarify this issue thoroughly.

First, let us discuss the relevant problem of whether we still continue to take the class struggle as the key link.

In leading our party in carrying out the socialist revolution, Chairman Mao's fundamental theory and practice for many years was to make the class struggle the key link. Chairman Mao continuously instructed us: "Never forget classes and the class struggle." In 1965 when Chairman Mao criticized Liu Shao-ch'i's revisionist line, he reiterated: "Class contradictions, class struggle between the proletariat and the bourgeoisie, and the two-way struggle between socialism and capitalism will exist throughout the transitional period. If we forget this more than ten-year-old fundamental theory and practice of our party, we shall go astray. Historical experience has taught us that to ignore or revise taking the class struggle as the key link inevitably leads to errors in theory and practice. In 1975 the intraparty capitalist roaders created the devilish whirlwind of rightist reversal of verdicts. While focusing on "the three directives as the key link," which had been advanced by a handful of intraparty unrepentant capitalist roaders led by Teng Hsiao-p'ing, Chairman Mao clearly expressed his views: "What is this talk of 'taking the three directives as the key link'? Stability and unity do not mean abandoning the class struggle; the class struggle is the key link, and everything else hinges on it."[1] After Chairman Mao passed away, the party's Central Committee, in the "Message to the Whole Party, the Whole Army, and the People of All Nationalities Throughout the Country," first of all pointed out that we must persevere in taking the class struggle as the key link. This is absolutely correct.

At present, the small, intraparty, counterrevolutionary, double-faced clique, with Hua Kuo-feng in control of the party's Central Committee, continuously pays lip service to the slogan of taking the class struggle as the key link. Do these fellows truly persevere in taking the class struggle as the key link? No. They outwardly pretend to do so, but inwardly they take Teng Hsiao-p'ing's "three directives as the key link."[2] The phrases used by Hua Kuo-feng and company — "taking the key link to govern the country," "great order to prevail soon," and "pushing the national economy forward" — are in essence carbon copies of Teng Hsiao-p'ing's so-called "promoting stability and unity" and "pushing the national economy forward." Yet Hua Kuo-feng and company are now vigorously polemicizing that since the Great Cultural Revolution "there has been talk only of politics, not of economics, talk only of revolution, not of production." This aptly reveals the similarity of their reactionary viewpoint to that previously declared by Teng Hsiao-p'ing and company in the so-called "On the General Program for All Work of the Whole Party and the Whole Country," and demonstrates their persistence in the revisionist "theory of sole reliance on productive force."[3]

Especially noteworthy is that more and more facts show that for Hua Kuo-feng and company the idea of class struggle is fundamentally not the class struggle in which the proletariat overthrow the bourgeoisie, but on the contrary a class struggle in which the bourgeoisie overthrow the proletariat. What these fellows want is not the dictatorship of the proletariat over the bourgeoisie, but on the contrary the dictatorship of the bourgeoisie over the proletariat. The object of their conspiracy is to transform proletarian political power into bourgeois political power.

The small, intraparty, counterrevolutionary, double-faced clique led by Hua Kuo-feng has used slander and incited controversy, steered [China] from one course to another, and adopted one stance in public while adopting another behind the public's back. Consequently during the past six months, our party has been led down the wrong road and rejected the class struggle as the key link.

After the death of Chairman Mao, the party's Central Committee in the "Message to the Whole Party, the Whole Army, and the People of All Nationalities Throughout the Country" set as the second most important item the "strengthening of the party's unified leadership and persevering in maintaining the party's unity and solidarity" in order to carry out the last will of Chairman Mao. But the small, intraparty, counterrevolutionary, double-faced clique never wanted party unity and solidarity. Within a month after Chairman Mao's death, a serious schism occurred within the party. The leading comrades Wang Hung-wen, Chang Chün-chiao, Chiang Ch'ing, and Yao Wen-yüan of the Central Committee were incarcerated by the small, intraparty, counterrevolutionary, double-faced clique led by Hua Kuo-feng. To give all comrades in the entire party a correct understanding of the incident, we feel it is imperative to express our opinion now.

On May 3, 1975, at a meeting of the Central Committee Politburo, Chairman Mao reiterated the basic principle of the "three do's and three don'ts." These were aimed at the small intraparty clique of unrepentant capitalist roaders lead by Teng Hsiao-p'ing, who, after the Fourth People's Congress [January 13–17, 1975], conspired to restore the reactionary essence of capitalism on the pretext of carrying out the Four Modernizations over the next 25 years. Chairman Mao warned them: "Do practice Marxism; don't practice revisionism. Do unite; don't split. Do be open and aboveboard; don't intrigue and conspire." This important directive of Chairman Mao not only strengthened the movement to learn the theory of proletarian dictatorship, but at the same time promoted efforts to maintain party unity and solidarity among all comrades in the entire party. These comrades conscientiously followed the party's basic line and policies during the historical stage of socialism; continuously criticized the counterrevolutionary revisionism of Liu Shao-ch'i and Lin Piao, capitalist tendencies, and the concept of bourgeois rights; and defended and developed the fruits of the victory of the Great Proletarian Cultural Revolution. With gladdened hearts and heightened emotions, we looked forward with complete confidence to achieving the great victory of the proletarian revolutionary line.

But who would have expected that Hua Kuo-feng and company would misconstrue the "three do's and three don'ts" of Chairman Mao, which referred to the conspiracy to restore capitalism by Teng Hsiao-p'ing and company, to represent Mao's "criticism" of the leading comrades, Wang Hung-wen, Chang Chün-chiao, Chiang Ch'ing, and Yao Wen-yüan of the party's Central Committee. Even Chairman Mao himself probably did not expect that after he died, the following phrases would be appended to his warning: "Don't function as a gang of four.

Don't do it. Why do you keep on doing so?" After incarcerating Wang, Chang, Chiang, and Yao, these fellows [Hua and company] perpetrated this heinous crime.

On October 6, 1976, while the whole party, the whole army, and the people of all nationalities throughout the country were undergoing the trauma of profound grief over Chairman Mao's death, Hua Kuo-feng and company, in a surprise coup, seditiously incarcerated the leading comrades Wang Hung-wen, Chang Chün-chiao, Chiang Ch'ing, and Yao Wen-yüan of the party's Central Committee. After several days of secret arrangements, Hua and company vigorously propagandized the "three do's and three don'ts" that had been stated by Chairman Mao and applied to the others the grand label of "practicing revisionism, schism, and conspiratorial trickery." This precipitate incident less than a month after Chairman Mao's death is ample proof that Hua Kuo-feng and company wasted little time and effort in taking over the party and seizing power. Judging from this incident, we can say that Hua Kuo-feng and company are really the ones practicing revisionism, schism, and conspiratorial trickery.

As for the "errors" allegedly committed by Wang Hung-wen, Chang Chün-chiao, Chaing Ch'ing and Yao Wen-yüan, we believe that every comrade in the entire party clearly understands that they were charged with these "errors" only after Hua Kuo-feng and company carried out a conspiracy to incarcerate Wang, Chang, Chiang, and Yao and deprived them of their right of speech by "first presuming them guilty before indicting them." Did Wang, Chang, Chiang, and Yao really "betray Marxism, Leninism, and the Thought of Mao Tse-tung, forge Chairman Mao's directives, practice revisionism, schism, and conspiratorial trickery, and recklessly attempt to usurp the supreme leadership of the party and country, subvert the proletarian dictatorship, and restore capitalism," as charged in the propaganda of Hua Kuo-feng and company? Up to now we have only the unilateral statement of Hua Kuo-feng and company. Some people will adjudge our remarks arbitrary. But no comrade in the party can overlook this fact: during the period of over twenty days from the decease of Chairman Mao to the seditious incarceration of Wang, Chang, Chiang, and Yao, there was no concrete fact that supports Hua Kuo-feng and company's allegation following the incarceration incident that Wang, Chang, Chiang, and Yao had "practiced revisionism, schism, and conspiratorial trickery." In addition, Hua Kuo-feng and company have never dared let Wang, Chang, Chiang, and

Yao make confessions before the masses, which suffices to prove the guilty conscience of these fellows [Hua and company].

Furthermore, from the time of the conspiracy to incarcerate Wang, Chang, Chiang, and Yao in October of last year [1976] to the present, Hua Kuo-feng and company have repeatedly listed numerous "errors" committed by Wang, Chang, Chiang, and Yao; yet all the incidents pointed out by them took place during Chairman Mao's lifetime. If this were true, wouldn't our wise, great leader and teacher, Chairman Mao, be a Liu A-tou?[4] Therefore, every comrade in the entire party will have no difficulty recognizing the evil activities of Hua Kuo-feng and company, who, instead of "singling out and criticizing the Gang of Four," have used the pretext of "singling out and criticizing the Gang of Four" to attack Chairman Mao in person. This is obviously a plot to try to kill two birds with one stone.

Especially serious is that after suddenly incarcerating Wang, Chang, Chiang, and Yao, Hua Kuo-feng and company have, on the basis of Hua's order "to expose and criticize deeply the remnants of the Gang of Four," indiscriminately attacked all those good, young comrades who, for the most part, joined the party since the Great Cultural Revolution and constituted over one-third of the total membership of the party, including revolutionary cadres in such basic units as the various government organs, army units, factories and mines, enterprises, shops, people's communes, schools, and streets throughout the country. These people not only have been arrested, oppressed, and wronged everywhere, but some good comrades who were sent overseas to engage in people's diplomacy and united front work also have been exposed, criticized, and attacked if they had any slight relationship with Wang, Chang, Chiang, and Yao. Isn't this an obvious case of practicing schism?

As a result of Hua Kuo-feng and company's deliberate practicing of revisionism, schism, and conspiratorial trickery and their destruction of party unity and solidarity, our party and country have once again fallen into a serious crisis involving a great schism and leap backward. If we fail to investigate this problem from various viewpoints, its external appearance will easily deceive us.

After conspiring to incarcerate the leading comrades, Wang Hung-wen, Chang Chün-chiao, Chiang Ch'ing, and Yao Wen-yüan of the party's Central Committee, Hua Kuo-feng and company tried to show that they were carrying out Chairman Mao's last will by implementing the affairs of the proletarian revolution. They decided on October 8,

1976, "to establish in the capital, Peking, a memorial hall for the great leader and teacher, Chairman Mao Tse-tung," to publish the *Selected Works of Mao Tse-tung*, and to prepare for the publication of the *Collected Works of Mao Tse-tung*. Along with the ground-breaking for Chairman Mao's memorial hall, volume 5 of the *Selected Works of Mao Tse-tung* was published and distributed in April of this year [1977]. But can Hua Kuo-feng and company really and seriously bear the burden of implementing the affairs of our proletarian revolution as handed down by Chairman Mao? Let us discuss this question here.

Every comrade in the whole party knows that the struggle to criticize Teng Hsiao-p'ing and to repulse the rightist reversal of verdicts was personally launched by Chairman Mao. After Chairman Mao's death, the party's Central Committee especially pointed out in the "Message to the Whole Party, the Whole Army, and the People of All Nationalities Throughout the Country":

> We must continue the behest bequeathed by Chairman Mao and con-solidate the great unity of the people of all nationalities under the lead-ership of the working class and, based on the worker-peasant alliance, deepen the criticism of Teng [Hsiao-p'ing], continue the struggle to re-pulse the rightist reversal of verdicts, consolidate and develop the fruits of the victory of the Great Proletarian Cultural Revolution, enthusiastically support the socialist newborn things, restrict bourgeois rights, and further consolidate the dictatorship of the proletariat in our country.

Carrying out Chairman Mao's proletarian revolutionary line is a great deed, which every comrade in our party must remember and thoroughly follow at all times and under all circumstances.

Since Hua Kuo-feng and company got control of the party's Central Committee, the criticism of Teng Hsiao-p'ing has been turned around [this was written before Teng's reinstatement in late 1977—tr.] That group has changed from seldom mentioning any criticism of Teng to never doing so. But it has also vigorously attacked those revolutionary comrades who insist on criticizing Teng and has absurdly stated that "criticism of Teng is really practicing something else." They have wrongly accused these comrades of "using the criticism of Teng as a pretext to assault comrade Hua Kuo-feng and other leading comrades of the party's Central Committee violently in order to usurp the party and seize power." They have made every attempt to defend Teng Hsiao-p'ing, both directly and indirectly. In recent months, an almost incredible event has occurred. Hua Kuo-feng and company have gone so far as to invoke repeatedly in their propaganda the Confucian saying, "Hear one's words and judge one by his deeds," that Teng Hsiao-p'ing quoted on October 29, 1975, during a speech before visiting German Federal Republic Chancellor Helmut Schmidt and his wife. This incident truly reveals that Hua Kuo-feng and company are basically not criticizing but praising Teng. At the same time, this incident also shows that these fellows do not criticize Confucius, but really behave in a reactionary way of venerating Confucius.

The small, intraparty, counterrevolutionary, double-faced clique led by Hua Kuo-feng ostensibly complied with but secretly violated Chairman Mao's directive to criticize Teng, so that in fact they really do not criticize Teng. Moreover, while repulsing the rightist reversal of verdicts, they pursue just the opposite path. Such reactionary films as *The Founding of An Enterprise, Rosy Clouds at Sea, The Song of the Gardener, The Great Wall on the South Sea,* and *Red Guards on Lake Hung* and local plays like *A Half Basket of Peanuts* and *The Morning Sun Ditch* have successively been revived during the past six months. These actions are ample testimony that Hua Kuo-feng and company not only have no intention of repulsing the rightist reversal of verdicts, but in fact propagate devilish, rightist reversal of verdicts. Meanwhile, these same fellows reveal themselves everywhere by not tackling the revisionist, reactionary line of Liu Shao-ch'i, Lin Piao, and Teng Hsiao-p'ing but, instead, opposing the proletarian revolutionary line of Chairman Mao. They are everywhere actively destroying the fruits of the victory gained in the Great Proletarian Cultural Revolution and strangling the newborn socialist things. What, indeed, is the purpose of their socialist revolution? Where should the spearhead of struggle be aimed? The relation between the enemy and ourselves has been completely reversed!

Hua Kuo-feng and company have used the method of pseudorevolution to oppose revolution, employed their pseudorevolutionary side to conceal their counterrevolutionary side, and utilized legality to disguise their illegality. Although Hua Kuo-feng wanted to establish a memorial hall for Chairman Mao and to publish Chairman Mao's works, and even though after the appearance of volume 5 of the *Selected Works of Mao Tse-tung,* Hua Kuo-feng especially wrote a long and self-glorifying treatise called "Continue the Revolution under the Dictatorship of the Proletariat to the End," we should not worship the rightist capitulationist line that he promoted by means of double-dealing conspiracies [disguised] as Chairman Mao's orthodox proletarian revolutionary line. If [we do] so, our whole party, the whole army, and the people of all nationalities throughout the country will commit a severe and irremediable blunder.

In December of last year and spring of this year, Hua Kuo-feng and company successively convened the Second National Conference on Learning from Tachai in Agriculture [December 10–27, 1976] and the National Conference on Learning from Taching in Industry [April 20– May 13, 1977]—two major events after these fellows seized the party's Central Committee. In order to enable all comrades in the entire party to understand thoroughly the reactionary nature of these two national conferences, we must also present our opinion here.

Within six months time, Hua Kuo-feng and company conceived of both the Second National Conference on Learning from Tachai in Agriculture and the National Conference on Learning from Taching in Industry. In their own words, these meetings constituted "a revolutionary mass movement to spread the learning from Tachai in agriculture and to popularize Tachai-type counties, and to learn from Taching in industry and to popularize Taching-type enterprises, in order to speed up industrial and agricultural development and to push the national economy forward." In calling these two conferences, did they truly wish "to speed up industrial and agricultural development and to push the national economy forward"? No! Absolutely not! Their real objectives were to implement on an extensive basis the reversal of verdicts and the restoration [of capitalism]. The so-called speeding up of industrial and agricultural development and pushing forward of the national economy merely served as the apparent reasons for their calling these two conferences; but their implementing on an extensive basis the reversal of verdicts and the restoration [of capitalism] on the industrial and agricultural fronts constituted the hidden reasons.

If we carry our observations one step further, it is not difficult to discover a characteristic common to both conferences. Both conferences, alike, stressed the campaign to "thoroughly expose and criticize the Gang of Four" on the production front; both emphasized their opposition to the interference of politics in business matters and production; both denied the excellence of developments since the Great Cultural Revolution.[5] If we connect these aspects, we can further reveal the reactionary nature of Hua Kuo-feng and company, who used these two conferences to practice revisionism, schism, and conspiratorial trickery.

The issue is extremely clear. During these two conferences, Hua Kuo-feng and company stressed the need to "thoroughly expose and criticize the Gang of Four." Their objective was to use on the industrial and agricultural fronts the pretext of "exposing and criticizing the remnants of the Gang of Four" to eliminate one revolutionary cadre after another in the various departments and units in order to regain the power that was taken away from the Liu [Shao-ch'i]/Teng [Hsiao-p'ing] clique of capitalist roaders on the industrial and agricultural fronts during the Great Cultural Revolution. Their objective was to implement the dictatorship of the bourgeoisie over the proletariat. Therefore, although Hua Kuo-feng and company kept shouting the phrase "take the class struggle as the key link" in these conferences, their so-called class struggle is a class struggle in which the bourgeoisie overthrow the proletariat.

As for these two conferences, Hua Kuo-feng and company reiterated their opposition to the interference of politics in business matters and production and denied the excellence of developments since the Great Cultural Revolution. Aside from these matters, which were closely related to the purge of personnel, their main objective was to carry out on an extensive basis the rightist reversal of verdicts and the restoration of capitalism. They stressed their opposition to the interference of politics in business matters and production as a pretext for reviving Liu Shao-ch'i's revisionist economic measures, such as the management of factories by experts, the primacy of technology, systematic versatility, material incentives, dictatorship of regulations, a foreign-slave philosophy, private plots, free markets, profits and losses on one's own account, and production contracts for each household. At the same time, these fellows denied the excellence of developments since the Great Cultural Revolution as a pretext for reversing the priorities of the class and production struggles. Thus they took up the revisionist mantle of Liu Shao-ch'i. On the production front, they revived and propagated the "theory of the withering of the class struggle" and the "theory of productivism," peddled the economic thought of the bourgeoisie, adopted the rightist capitulationist line, and opposed Chairman Mao's proletarian revolutionary line.

Lenin stated: "Politics must precede economics." Not to affirm this point is to forget the most basic knowledge of Marxism." What is politics here? Lenin has succinctly said: "Politics is the struggle between various classes." To forget the class struggle, or to place the class struggle in a secondary position, or even, on the contrary, to interpret the class strug-

gle maliciously as a class struggle in which the bourgeoisie overthrow
the proletariat is to sidetrack socialist construction. Undoubtedly, the
two conferences conceived by Hua Kuo-feng and company utterly opposed the principle of "we should continue to unfold the three great
revolutionary movements of class struggle, the struggle for production,
and scientific experiment"—which the party's Central Committee advanced after the death of Chairman Mao in the "Message to the Whole
Party, the Whole Army, and the People of All Nationalities Throughout
the Country."

Moreover, an incident that should serve as a special warning to every
comrade in the entire party occurred on May 4 of this year during the
National Conference on Learning from Taching in Industry. The party's
Central Committee, which had been manipulated by Hua Kuo-feng and
company, entrusted Yu Ch'iu-li, a ruthless leader of the Liu-Teng counterrevolutionary clique, to present a report to all delegates attending this
conference. The subject matter of the report included the fighting tasks
for the entire party and the working classes throughout the country. All
delegates attending this conference had to study this report seriously,
which should prove its significance. But all comrades in the whole
party know that before the Great Cultural Revolution, Yu Ch'iu-li was
an important member of the black gang that promoted Liu Shao-ch'i's
revisionist, enterprise-management line in opposition to Chairman Mao's
revolutionary line. He is an unrepentant, old-time capitalist roader. Why
was this scoundrel allowed to present an important report at the National Conference on Learning from Taching in Industry? Why was this
member of the black gang permitted to show his importance and display
his power? Striking down revolutionary comrades one after another and
permitting such evil persons to acquire eminence are the specialties of
Hua Kuo-feng and company.

Since Hua Kuo-feng and company used the two conferences to practice revisionism, schism, and conspiratorial trickery, these conferences
gave these fellows an audience in front of whom to parade monsters
and demons. Disastrous consequences may result interminably.

Having examined these facts clearly, we find it easy to reach the following conclusion. After the party's Central Committee was taken over
by the small, intraparty, counterrevolutionary, double-faced clique
led by Hua Kuo-feng, who with open mouth has screamed the Thought
of Mao Tse-tung but has committed criminal acts behind everyone's
back against the party, socialism, and the Thought of Mao Tse-tung,

our party no longer follows the proletarian revolutionary line. It is following the rightist capitulationist line. Since this ironclad case against them is as weighty as a mountain, we shall never allow them to lie again!

During the course of the Great Cultural Revolution when Wang Hung-wen, Chang Chün-chiao, Chiang Ch'ing, and Yao Wen-yüan rose up brazenly to heaven, haughtily treading on everyone's rights and isolating themselves from the masses, they certainly had no sufficient cause for success but ample grounds for disaster. But Hua Kuo-feng is basically a turncoat dragon, as well as the counterrevolutionary double-dealer par excellence. Chi Teng-kuei is merely a secondhand counterrevolutionary double-dealer. In addition, Yeh Chien-ying is just an old warlord. Ch'en Hsi-lien and Hsü Shih-yu are but little warlords. Teng Hsiao-p'ing is an unrepentant capitalist roader. If these persons are allowed to seize the party's Central Committee and the State Council, our party will sooner or later become revisionist and our country will change color!

Since Chairman Mao's death, the heavy burden of the proletarian revolution has fallen on the shoulders of the younger generation in our party. Every young comrade in our whole party must thoroughly expose all the relevant facts about the conspiracies relating to Hua Kuo-feng and company's betrayal of Marxism, Leninism, and the Thought of Mao Tse-tung, their restoration of capitalism, and their subversion of the proletarian dictatorship, in order to speak the truth everywhere. Every young Communist party member and Communist Youth League member should further swear to carry high the red banner of the Thought of Mao Tse-tung forever. They must persist in taking the class struggle as the key link, follow the party's basic line, and continue the revolution under the dictatorship of the proletariat so that we may direct the spearhead of struggle against Hua Kuo-feng and company and sweep away into the garbage bin of history all monsters and demons of any size who have betrayed the party and the country.

THE SHANGHAI MUNICIPAL
COMMITTEE OF THE COMMUNIST
YOUTH LEAGUE

Eve of the 56th Anniversary
of the Founding of the
Communist Party of China
[June 30, 1977]

Pledge to Carry Out
the Proletarian Revolution to the End

(The People's Press, Kiangsi, ca. October 1977)

DOCUMENT FOUR

課 The great revolutionary teacher, Chairman Mao, wisely predicted before passing away that a handful of careerists and conspirators would definitely engage in an anticommunist, rightist coup d'etat after his death. For this reason, he addressed a very grave warning to them, stating that they must fulfill the "three correct dealings," that is, "to deal correctly with the Great Proletarian Cultural Revolution, to deal correctly with the masses, and to deal correctly with themselves." His purpose was to guide them enthusiastically onto the correct path based on the policy of "learning from past mistakes to avoid future ones and curing the sickness to save the patient," in order to spare them the disgraceful fate of incurring irreparable damage to their bodies and reputations or even of death.

But this handful of persons, in their stupid, obstinate, and unrepentant ways, are even more ferocious and treacherous than wolves that wish to kill when hungry and to fight when full. Within a month after Chairman Mao's death, they were malicious enough to launch a sudden raid and to illegally arrest the leading comrades who had persisted in Chairman Mao's great revolutionary line. Thus, they totally negated the principles and policies of the Great Proletarian Cultural Revolution. They were disorderly and clamorous and viciously trampled on legal rights; wherever their henchmen went, tragedy and carnage ensued. The massacres extended from Paoting, Wenchow, Chin-chiang, and Nanchang to all parts of the nation and have increasingly become more extensive and brutal. What they call "taking the key link to govern the country" is, in fact, a thoroughly criminal act that destroys our laws and damages our nation.

As real gold does not fear a roaring fire in a furnace, so it is easy to determine if a revolution is genuine or phony.

On the basis of factual proof, it is well known to all that Chairman Mao personally proposed, and the Politburo of the party's Central Committee unanimously approved, the dismissal of Teng Hsiao-p'ing from all posts both inside and outside the party. Even members of your clique [the present leaders] who have usurped control of the party, seized power, and divided the spoils by wheeling and dealing, clamored during the first few months to carry out the struggle of "criticizing Teng and opposing the right" to the end. But no sooner had you wagged your foxtails [practiced deception] than you pronounced Chairman Mao's directive a "forgery" and claimed that Teng Hsiao-p'ing was "framed." If you continue to act in such a preposterous way, all the great and wise directives of Chairman Mao will be proclaimed "phony" except for the so-called memorandum declaring, "With you in charge, I am at ease," which you certainly forged!

Communists neither believe in demons nor fear devils. But you handful of careerists and conspirators who have taken over the party and confused the country never hold the truth in your hands or have the support of the masses. Under these extremely isolated and fearful conditions, you have nevertheless served up a large number of decadent specters who opposed Chairman Mao during his lifetime and even assailed the Great Cultural Revolution. Although their ideology still stagnates alongside that of the former warlords and old bureaucrats of the democratic revolutionary era, they swagger through the streets, posing as gods and demons. You are interested only in using these specters as your "guards." Moreover, you have already forgotten Chairman Mao's teaching that our revolution must forever march forward and have even cast it by the wayside and stomped on it once more!

The most important aspect of the Great Cultural Revolution was its ideological revolution. We must understand the universal truth of Marxism-Leninism correctly and thoroughly reform our world views so that the phenomenon of bourgeoisie-dominated ideology will be basically altered to revert to proletariat-dominated ideology. But you handful of heartless, maniacal, depraved persons are truly birds of a feather. While you have not yet settled yourselves in your jobs, you are already busily engaged in proclaiming amnesty for rebels and receiving renegades, which means, in effect, rescuing one by one the many drowning dogs that had been eternally condemned during the Great Cultural Revolution. These people were not only given official posts and promoted in rank, but were also sent to write essays and to form a monstrous and demonic chorus of capitalist roaders. These persons have created a devilish whirlwind by twisting, splitting, and even rejecting Chairman Mao's great revolutionary theory. By so doing, you have not merely become revisionist and changed in character, but you have become renegades and traitors, as well as repugnant, stinking dog droppings.

You have ruthlessly suppressed all revolutionary youths, especially the revolutionary young intellectuals, who dared to rebel and turn back the tide running against the Great Cultural Revolution. You handful of careerists and conspirators have extensively persecuted and massacred those cadres and members of all local labor unions, poor and lower-middle peasant organizations, the Communist Youth League, the Women's Association, and urban and rural militia who are more persistent [than you] in carrying out Chairman Mao's great and correct revolutionary line and more successful in making their contributions to the party and the people. The revolutionaries are now "guilty," and the restorationists are "back at home." Doesn't this prove the class characteristics of your anticommunist coup d'etat?

Liu Shao-ch'i established [shortly after 1949] the "commissions for inspecting discipline" at various levels of party committees in order to carry out his personal "monolithic" organizational control; Lin Piao implemented the abominable means of "assaulting a great mass and protecting a small handful" [of people] as his magic weapon for seizing and defending power. Now you not merely imitate them point by point but surpass them time and again.[1] You do not allow others to turn back the tide, but establish a thoroughgoing dictatorship for the sake of making all 800 million Chinese people an "instrument of your slavery." You, Liu Shao-ch'i, Lin Piao, and other renegades, traitors, scamps, and counterrevolutionary groups, are totally all alike in words and deeds. But we dare to speak out so that all renegades opposed to Marxism-Leninism and the Thought of Mao Tse-tung will eventually end in fiasco and disgrace—just like Liu Shao-ch'i, Lin Piao, and others like them. This will certainly happen.

In history, new and correct things can develop only out of struggle—in a zigzag manner. Under the wise guidance of our great leader, Chairman Mao, our party has, through the ten struggles about the [correct] line, amply proved this point. The reactionary cliques are indeed grandiloquent, omnipresent, and conceited at times, and they frequently overestimate their own strength and underestimate our revolutionary strength. But the people's eyes are as clear as ice, while dregs float, demons trick, jackals and wolves roam over the road, and snakes and rats run wild. All this is no more than a transitory phenomenon, for the country wants progress and the people want revolution. These, then, are the motive forces in history.

Chairman Mao said long ago: "If an anticommunist, rightist coup d'etat develops in China, I assert that they [the participants] will not be able to rest in peace and will possibly last only for a short time because the revolutionaries, who represent over 90 percent of the interests of the people, will never be able to tolerate them." Chairman Mao also taught: "In dealing with the struggle against a rightist, we shall let him rave for a while to the extreme, then he will dig his own grave." At present, they have already reached the height of their craze, and the eleventh struggle about the [correct] line of our party is also the struggle of our whole party, our whole army, and the people of all nationalities throughout the country against the handful of remnants of capitalist roaders, consisting of Hua [Kuo-feng], Yeh [Chien-ying], Teng [Hsiao-p'ing], Li [Hsien-nien], and Wang [Tung-hsing]. This must be carried out by us, who are of a younger generation and dare to turn back the tide with even greater unity and determination than if we were riding herd on thousands of galloping horses, overthrowing a mountain, or upending the sea.

"Radiant with the morning sun, the heart fears nothing; [we are] determined to oppose revisionism and fight the evil wind." For the sake of realizing the last will of the great leader, Chairman Mao, and exonerating and redressing the grievances of thousands of class brethren, revolutionary comrades, and comrades-in-arms who have been persecuted, we are resolved not to fear any difficulties or sacrifices; and we take an oath to trample underfoot all obstacles that block our revolutionary path and completely bury all heinous enemies both within and without the party.

While the earth revolves, we will continue to wage our struggle. We pledge to carry out the Chinese proletarian revolution to the end and to create a beautiful tomorrow from our labors.

THE GREAT CRITICISM SECTION
OF THE KIANGSI COMMUNIST
LABOR UNIVERSITY OF THE
October 20, 1977   COMMUNIST PARTY OF CHINA

Notes

The following abbreviations are used in the notes:

HC   Hung-ch'i (Red Flag)
JMJP Jen-min jih-pao (People's Daily)
PR   Peking Review (Beijing Review)

INTRODUCTION

1. *PR* Jan. 24, 1975, pp. 23–24.

2. As pronounced by Chou En-lai in June 1954 at New Delhi, the five principles of peaceful coexistence are: mutual respect for each other's territorial integrity, nonaggression, nonintervention in each other's internal affairs, equality and mutual respect, and peaceful coexistence.

3. "Communiqué of the Third Plenum of the Central Committee, July 21, 1977," *PR* July 29, 1977, pp. 3–8.

4. "Glorious Mission of the Chinese Youth," *PR* Nov. 17, 1978, pp. 8, 10.

5. "How the 'Gang of Four' Used Shanghai as a Base to Usurp Party and State Power," *PR* Feb. 4, 1977, p. 7.

6. "Failure of 'Gang of Four's' Scheme to Set Up a 'Second Armed Force,'" *PR* Mar. 25, 1977, p. 12.

7. For text, see *HC* 1976, no. 10 (Sept.): 5–9; and *PR* Sept. 13, 1976, pp. 6–11.

8. Teng's "three directives," consisting of (1) studying the theory of proletarian dictatorship, (2) stability and unity, and (3) pushing the national economy forward, were issued in late 1975, allegedly under Chairman Mao's instructions between 1964 and 1974.

9. "On the General Program," "Some Problems Concerning the Work of Science and Technology," and "Some Problems in Accelerating Industrial Development" (all dated 1975) constitute what were known as the "three big poisonous weeds," according to the Gang of Four. For details, see the editorial "Grasp the Crucial Point and Deepen the Criticism of Teng Hsiao-p'ing," *JMJP* Aug. 23, 1976, p. 1; and *PR* Aug. 27, 1976, pp. 5–6.

10. "Vice Premier Teng Hsiao-p'ing's Speech," *PR* Nov. 7, 1975, p. 7.

11. This title was translated in the original document as "PLEDGED TO CARRY THROUGH THE PROLETARIAT REVOLUTION TO THE END."

12. "How the 'Gang of Four' Used Shanghai," p. 8.

13. *JMJP* Aug. 7, 1958, p. 9.

14. *JMJP* Aug. 11, 1971, p. 1.

15. *JMJP* Aug. 14, 1975, p. 2.

16. For Teng's dismissal, see "Resolution of C.P.C. Central Committee on Dismissing Teng Hsiao-p'ing from All Posts Both Inside and Outside the Party," *PR* Apr. 9, 1976, p. 3.

17. This memorandum was allegedly addressed by Chairman Mao to Hua Kuo-feng on Apr. 30, 1976. See "Comrade Wu Teh's Speech at the Celebration Rally in the Capital," *HC* 1976, no. 11 (Nov.): 18; and *PR* Oct. 29, 1976, p. 12. But the memorandum is not mentioned in Hua Kuo-feng's "Political Report to the Eleventh National Congress of the Communist Party of China," delivered on Aug. 12, 1977. See "Political Report," *HC* 1977, no. 9 (Sept.): 3–31; and *PR* Aug. 26, 1977, pp. 23–57.

18. On setting up commissions for inspecting discipline, see "Constitution of the Communist Party of China" (adopted by the Eleventh National Congress of the CPC on Aug. 18, 1977), chap. 2, art. 13. See *HC* 1977, no. 9 (Sept.): 37; and *PR* Sept. 2, 1977, p. 21. It is significant to note that according to a Reuters report dated Dec. 23, 1978, from Peking, the Third Plenum of the Eleventh Central Committee, which was convened during December 18–22, created a "Central Commission for Inspecting Discipline," headed by the newly elected Vice-Chairman Ch'en Yün of the party and consisting of over one hundred members, including many communist leaders who were purged before and during the Cultural Revolution.

19. *Time,* Jan. 1, 1979.

20. According to *Newsweek,* "The invasion of Vietnam has produced the first stirrings of an 'antiwar movement' in major Chinese cities. . . . But the posters on Democracy Wall [in the capital] are only the most visible part of what one American in Peking calls 'a full-blown dissident movement.'" [See "China's Antiwar Movement," *Newsweek,* Mar. 12, 1979, p. 36.]

21. For a treatment of this subject, see Peter R. Moody, *Opposition and Dissent in Contemporary China* (Stanford: Hoover Institution Press, 1977).

DOCUMENT ONE

1. All the events under attack occurred after the deterioration of Sino-Russian relations in the late 1950s.

2. According to this document, Mao alleged that he had been compelled by Lin Piao to commit illegal acts against others.

3. The Four Purities movement concerned economy, politics, organization, and thought, as part of the Socialist Education movement (1962–66).

4. This criticism is as unfavorable to Kuomintang as to Chinese Communist rule.

5. According to Chou En-lai's report at the first session of the Third National People's Congress, December 22, 1964, some people in 1959–1962 wanted a reconciliation with the imperialists, reactionaries, and modern revisionists and a reduction in aid to other people in revolt.

6. This is the document's sole reference to "Soviet revisionist social-imperialism."

7. This quotation comes from the famous novel, *Dream of the Red Chamber.*

8. The so-called "Central Extraordinary Committee" was first formed as a rightist group on January 31, 1931, at Shanghai, under the leadership of Lo Chang-lung, with branches planned in Chekiang, Kiangsu, Hupei, Hopei, and Manchuria. This group began to disintegrate in early April that year.

DOCUMENT TWO

1. Literally, "Proletarians of the Whole World, Unite!"

2. For the five principles of coexistence, see note 2 to the Introduction. As enunciated by Chou En-lai when touring Africa in 1964, the eight principles are: (1) equality and mutual benefit, (2) respect for sovereignty and independence of recipients, (3) interest-free or low-interest loans, (4) self-reliance and independent economic development for recipients, (5) low-investment and quick-result projects, (6) high-quality equipment and material of Chinese manufacture, (7) requirement of full ability on the part of recipients to benefit from special technical assistance, and (8) the same standard of living for Chinese technicians as that of their counterparts in the recipient country. For details, see the text of Chou En-lai's speech at the Mogadishu mass rally, *PR* Feb. 14, 1964, p. 8.

3. A famous quotation from Han Yü (768–824), an outstanding statesman and writer.

4. Literally: ". . . and the Americans came breaking wind and pissing in fear."

5. Chia Kuei was the trusted lackey of a Ming dynasty eunuch, Liu Chin.

6. *Apotheosis of Heroes* is a popular Chinese mythological novel.

DOCUMENT THREE

1. For text, see "Message to the Whole Party, the Whole Army, and the People of All Nationalities Throughout the Country," *PR* Sept. 13, 1976, p. 10.

2. For details of the controversy, see the editorial "Embrace Class Struggle, Promote Spring Farming," *JMJP* Feb. 24, 1976, p. 1; and *PR* Mar. 5, 1976, p. 5. For the "three directives," see note 8 to the Introduction.

3. For further information, see the editorial "Grasp the Crucial Point and Deepen the Criticism of Teng Hsiao-p'ing," *JMJP* Aug. 23, 1976, p. 1; and *PR* Aug. 27, 1976, p. 5. "On the General Program for All Work of the Whole Party and the Whole Country" was one of the so-called "three big antiparty and anti-Marxist poisonous weeds."

4. An inept ruler, 223–263 A.D., of the Shu-Han dynasty.

5. See the editorial "Thoroughly Expose and Criticize the 'Gang of Four,'" *JMJP* Nov. 28, 1976, p. 1; and *PR* Dec. 3, 1976, p. 6.

DOCUMENT FOUR

1. The 1977 constitution of the Communist Party of China set up the commissions for inspecting discipline; see chap. 2, art. 13. See *HC* 1977, no. 9 (Sept.): 37; and *PR* Sept. 2, 1977, p. 21. The First Plenum of the commission, presided over by Vice-Chairman Ch'en Yün of the party as first secretary, took place in Peking January 4–22, 1979. See "Communiqué of the Third Plenum of the Eleventh Central Committee of the Communist Party of China," *PR* Dec. 29, 1978, pp. 7–8; and *HC* 1979, no. 1 (Jan.): 14–15. See also "Events and Trends," *PR* Feb. 9, 1979, pp. 5–6.

Index